EGALITARIAN TYPOLOGIES
VERSUS THE
PERCEPTION OF THE UNIQUE

James Hillman

Spring Publications, Inc.
Dallas, Texas

Published by Spring Publications, Inc.; P.O. Box 222069; Dallas, Texas 75222
Printed in the United States of America

Cover design and production by Maribeth Lipscomb and Patricia Mora

International Distributors
Spring; Postfach; 8800 Thalwil; Switzerland
Japan Spring Sha, Inc.; 1-2-4, Nishisakaidani-Cho; Ohharano, Nishikyo-Ku; Kyoto, 610-11, Japan
Element Books Ltd; Longmead; Shaftesbury Dorset SP7 8PL; England

Library of Congress Cataloging-in-Publication Data

Hillman, James.
    Egalitarian typologies versus the perception of
the unique.

    ''Lecture presented originally at the 1976 Eranos
Conference, in Ascona, Switzerland, and appeared in
the Eranos yearbook, 45, 1976''—T.p. verso.
    Includes bibliographical references.
    1. Typology (Psychology)—Congresses.   2. Jung, C. G.
(Carl Gustav), 1875-1961—Congresses.   I. Title.
BF698.H485   1986   155.2'64   85-26160
ISBN 0-88214-404-9

Eranos Lectures series: ISSN 0743-586X

Acknowledgments
''Egalitarian Typologies *versus* the Perception of the Unique'' was a lecture
presented originally at the 1976 Eranos Conference in Ascona, Switzerland, and
appeared in the *Eranos Yearbook* 45—1976 (Ascona: Eranos Foundation,
1980), pp. 221-80. It is published here with the kind permission of the Eranos
Foundation.

CONTENTS

The Eranos Lectures Series

I. *Persons as Types*

„*Esse* is *percipi*"
George Berkeley, *Of the Principles
of Human Knowledge*, I, 3.

Three persistent irritations have urged me to this topic. Perhaps you will understand the topic better if I can portray the irritations. The first has to do with elitism. Nature, said Jung, is aristocratic and esoteric (*CW 11*, §537; *7*, §198). It is profligate; only few events come to birth, far fewer to full flowering. Jungians are concerned with these rare events, the opus of individuation, working on one's individuality so as to be wholeheartedly all that one is. This requires differentiation (by which word Jung defines individuation — *CW 6* §§ 755, 757, 761), elaborating differences within oneself and between oneself and others. This stress upon the *differentness* of individual personality and the private modes of its development means that an avowed Jungian suffers the charge of elitism. So, our first problem is how to work with individual uniqueness without at the same time becoming elitist. This problem must be met by every Platonist man of the spirit who at the same time would be a democratic citizen and polytheistic liberal in soul. One way of attempting the dilemma is to examine the other side of elitist fantasy, i.e., egalitarianism.

The second thorn has to do with Jung's *Psychological Types*. As you know, this work — begun over sixty years ago — is that part of his opus most well-known to the public, and it is being revived today by many Jungians in hopes of putting their school on a more clinical, or scientific, or academic basis. I for one feel profoundly discomfited by Jung's typology — and even more by a science of personality based on a scientific method of types. Once the label has been found, the inferiority or superiority identified, then what? How does one imagine further? Moreover, is it not the old drill-sergeant Ego who is called on to develop the raw and lazy inferiorities by marching the mandala round through all four functions.

My irritation seems supported by other Jungian analysts. In an international survey published in 1972 on the use of typology among Jungians in active practice, result number one states: "only half the number of analysts replying found the typology helpful in analytical practice"[1]. But surely we cannot so lightly dismiss Jung's major work of his middle period. What relevance has Jung's typology? Why types at all?

Before we proceed into the third worry, there is, curiously enough, a direct connection between egalitarianism and typology right within Jung's book. I am referring to the last few pages, the Epilogue which opens with "Liberté, Egalité, Fraternité" (§ 845), the cry of the French Revolution whose "egalitarian reforms" Jung praises. But social and political equality Jung clearly distinguishes from psychological egalitarianism, saying: "No social legislation will ever be able to overcome the psychological differences between men" and he finds it serves "a useful purpose therefore to speak of the heterogeneity of men". His *Types* was conceived to elaborate differences, variety. Yet, the Epilogue, like a foreboding afterthought, points to what has since happened: the book has become an instrument of psychological egalitarianism by means of typical categories into which persons can be fit. Instead of helping us to relativize all psychological positions, it establishes them more fixedly. The book has converted into its opposite: it has become an instrument of the egalitarianism it is expressly designed to ward off, and a more insidious kind — psychological egalitarianism. But we shall come back to Jung in more detail later.

Now, the problem of perceiving the unique. This problem is at the heart of therapy. For, if there is one thing each patient needs,

---

[1] A. Plaut, "Analytical Psychologists and Psychological Types", *J. Analyt. Psychol.* 17/2, 1972, p. 143.

it is to be perceived in his or her uniqueness, and if there is one thing an analyst struggles with unrelentingly, it is to espy a particular and different self in each patient. The desire to see and the need to be seen cannot be overestimated; when such seeing and being seen takes place, it is like a blessing.[2] Despite what is revealed of a patient's psychodynamics, the typical and archetypal patterns of interior life and the soul's history, until I can envisage this person's uniqueness I cannot imagine him profoundly enough and therefore cannot recognize who he is. I see individuation but not individuality. If my work is with an empirical embodied self in its individuality, then how perceive a self, not in symbols and synchronicities, not hermeneutically, but immediately in the person before my eyes, concrete and present.

My misgiving here seems a widespread malaise. The clinician takes few cues from the *kline* (bedside). Instead, he reads blood tests. He is trained to see in groups and typings, a taxonomic eye that coordinates with a prescriptive hand dispensing treatments. A person written about in a case report is far less enunciated than one finds in a novel or biography. Psychiatry texts, today swollen to obesity, are crammed with statistics. But where are the careful descriptions of ill persons, such as we find in Krafft-Ebing and Eugen Bleuler. When I attend discussions on candidate selection for analytical training, I am abused by the banal descriptions and unawareness of character in the remarks of my colleagues — and in my own. Something has happened to the sight of the psychologist, and owing to our gradual glaucoma we turn more and more to committees, objective tests, increased quantities of training. The problem of uniqueness is not merely methodological — the old argument between nomothetic and idiographic, between statistical, experimental psychology *versus* clinical, between science *versus*

---

[2] "Blessing" might also be put as "healing", in that what is required is an insight into essential nature, a *seeing*. When Paracelsus refuses the first Hippocratic aphorism (art is long, life short), he says this is so only for the poor physician because he is looking (or empirically searching), which is not seeing. The true physician must see the illness as the geometer sees the circle — an imaginative act. L. Braun, "Paracelse, Commentateur des *Aphorismes* d'Hippocrate", *La Collection Hippocratique et son rôle dans l'histoire de la médicine*, Leiden: Brill, 1975, p. 345.

nomathetic -

art in psychology.[3] The problem is rather *the* problem of human relations: the experiencing of each other as selves, as individual persons with distinct natures; each person the embodiment of an individual destiny.

How did others do it in other times? So much has depended upon the ability to see the nature of the person before our eyes. For instance at the French Court in the 1850's and 60's the German, Austrian, British, and Russian Ambassadors each sent back their reports based on their readings of the enigmatic, ill and capricious Napoleon the Third. Cowley, the British Ambassador, read best and what he said was best in tune with historical events. How did General Haig grasp his French colleagues on the Western Front or decide upon appointments for Commanders of its sections — Haig, who is usually considered a military ramrod, a wholly unpsychological John Bull. Yet his biographers show his concisely summing up character on which terrible decisions rested after the briefest encounter with a previously unknown person. How does a baseball scout perceive the uniqueness in a nineteen-year-old rookie in-fielder in the bush leagues, size him up not only in terms of skills, but see a nature that will fit him into a team and be worth long investment of money and time?

Let me tell you three stories: At Harvard in the 1890's Professor William James had in his classes a rather wonky, stubby talkative Jewish girl from California. She was late for classes, didn't seem to understand what was going on, misspelled, knew no Latin — that sort of typical mess, the girl who couldn't get it together, a "typical neurotic" as we might say today. But William James let her turn in a blank

---

[3] G. W. Allport's writings are the most sympathetic to this division; in fact, he has been accused of causing it. See, R. R. Holt, "Individuality and Generalization in the Psychology of Personality", *J. Pers.* 30, 1962, pp. 377–404. Also, P. E. Meehl, *Clinical vs. Statistical Prediction*, Minneapolis: Univ. Minn. Press, 1954; G. W. Allport, "The General and the Unique in Psychological Science", *J. Pers.* 30, 1962, pp. 405–22, where Allport proffers the term "morphogenic" to replace idiographic for study of the individual, a term drawing attention to visible shape. The tendency of psychologists (noticed by both Holt and Allport) to misspell *idiographic* as *ideographic* also suggests an unconscious assimilation of uniqueness by conceptual ideation.

exam paper, and gave her a high mark for the course, helped her through to medical studies at Johns Hopkins. He saw something unique in this pupil. She was Gertrude Stein, who found herself as the Gertrude Stein we know only ten years later far from Harvard, in Paris.

In a Southern small town a man named Phil Stone, who had some literary education at Yale, took under his wing as coach and mentor, a short, wiry, heavily drinking, highly pretentious lad of the town. This young fellow wrote poems, pretended to be British, carried a walking stick and wore special clothes — all in smalltown Mississippi during the First World War. Phil Stone listened to the boy, whom we might call today a "typical puer" and perceived his uniqueness. The man went on to become the William Faulkner who was awarded the Nobel Prize for literature in 1949. A third tale of the perception of uniqueness: In the year 1831 one of those marvellous old-fashioned scientific expeditions was to set forth; a schoolmaster named John Henslow suggested that one of his former pupils be appointed naturalist. The lad was then 22; he had been rather dull at school, hopeless in maths, although a keen collector of beetles from the countryside; he was hardly different from the others of his type and class: hunting and shooting, popular member of the Glutton Club aimed for the clergy. He had a "typical family complex" as we might say today, soft in the mother and dominated by a 300-pound father. But Henslow saw something and persuaded the parties involved, including the pupil named Charles Darwin, that he make his journey.

What did they see and how did they see it? Is this sort of seeing a special gift, as some have held, or is it possible to anyone — providing nothing stands in the way of such perception, a perception which implies, in these cases, a deep subjective affection, a loving.

Now, here we can detect an inter-relation between two of our problems. For what might have stood in the way of seeing uniqueness could have been seen typically — to have seen Gertrude Stein as a typical neurotic girl, William Faulkner as a typical puer, Charles Darwin as a typical family-boy, with an obsessive hobby but not much 'upstairs'. Had we seen by means of modern psychology, that is, typicalities, we could have missed the target.

There is also a relation with our other problem, egalitarianism. The sort of perception we just described singled out Stein, Faulkner, and Darwin. The eye that saw them saw them differently and in their differences.

Hearing these tales of Stein, Faulkner, and Darwin, or rather of James, Stone, and Henslow, we could make a psychological maxim of Berkeley's principle: *esse* is *percipi*. To be is to be perceived. Stein, Faulkner, and Darwin become what they were because of having been perceived. Their being was the result, in part, of that being having been perceived.

But first we turn to what might get in the way of such perception — types, and the concept of types. Then we turn to modes other than types for the perception of persons.

The Type Concept[4]: The word *typos* does not quite mean *Schlag* or *blow* as we have been taking for granted. Originally, the way *typos* was used in Greek gave it the meaning of an empty or hollow form for casting, a kind of rough-edged mold. From the beginning of its use by Plato and Aristotle the word had a sketchy, incomplete relief, or outline character that emphasizes a visible shaping quality rather than a sharply struck definition.[5] Even today in modern logic and epistemology, a type differs from other ordering categories just by virtue of its imprecision.

---

[4] For the concept and theories of "types", see: W. Ruttkowski, *Typologie und Schichtenlehre* (a descriptive international bibliography, with index, until 1970) Amsterdam: Rodopi N. V., 1974; C. G. Hempel & P. Oppenheim, *Der Typusbegriff im Lichte der neuen Logik*, Leiden: Sijthoff, 1936; A. Koort, "Beiträge zur Logik des Typusbegriffs", *Acta et Comment. Univ. Tartu* (Finland), Bde. 38–39; I, 1–138, II, 139–263, 1936–38; A. Seiffert, "Die kategoriale Stellung des Typus" *Beiheft z. Zeitschrift f. philos. Forschung*, Meisenheim/Glan: Anton Hain, 1953; W. A. Lessa, "An Appraisal of Constitutional Typologies", *American Anthropologist* (n.s.) 45,4:2, 1943, pp. 7–96; Otto Schindewolf, „Über den 'Typus' in morphologischer und phylogenetischer Biologie", *Akad. d. Wissenschaften u. Literatur: Mathem.-Naturwiss. Klasse* 1969:4, Weisbaden: Franz Steiner, 1969.
[5] A. von Blumenthal, *"Typos* und *Paradeigma"*, *Hermes* 63, 1928, pp. 391–414 & contra the etymology of Liddell & Scott.

Owing to this uncertain boundary, types are used most frequently in life-sciences and humanities. Types can flow into one another: there is no sharp border between typical historical periods (Mediaeval and Renaissance), between typical literary styles (heroic and tragic), or between typical groupings of mental disorders, social functions or even animal species. Fluidity, relativity, elasticity is a most distinctive aspect of the type concept.

Therefore, there cannot be any pure types because they are not meant to be pure, by definition.[6] A pure type has already become a class where a different sort of logic obtains. My name begins with H, and I was called to military service in 1944. That puts me into two classes with hard edges. There is nothing typical about persons whose names begin with H or who were called up in 1944. We can, however, be classified with H and 44. Classes require an 'either/or', types a 'more/less', kind of thinking. I am either an H or I am not; I cannot be more of an H than an L or a T, or a lesser H or a little H, etc. But with types I am rather more an extravert than an introvert, a point which Jung made at the very beginning of his *Psychological Types* (§§ 4–6). Extraversion does not *per se* exclude introversion.

---

[6] The very impurity of types in experience therefore necessitates "ideal" types (Dilthey, Jaspers, Spranger, Max Weber) which are not intended to be evidentially verified, but which are required as purely imagined backgrounds for understanding human experience. Ideal types are like Platonic ideas (but denied their metaphysical implications — A. Rustow, "Der Idealtypus, oder die Gestalt als Norm", *Stud. Generale* 6/1, 1953, p. 54). But ideal types are unlike Platonic ideas because the way in which they are formed gives them a freakish, caricature-like quality. They are constructed by intensifying, exaggerating, and purifying singular traits at the expense of others and subsuming those others within the salient ideal type as a Gestalt. They exist in no single instance, and are thus unnatural — which is precisely their value for seeing through the natural. The act which forms an ideal type is a *Wesenschau*, an insight into essence, and not a statistical averaging (norms) or a logical reasoning (classes). Neither empirical nor logical methods apply. Rustow (p. 59) calls the principle by which they are formed "morphological". Ideal types require an imagination of Gestalten or forms. Jung's types belong here inasmuch as they are an imagined morphology of consciousness, a phenomenology of the shapes of experience. For examples of ideal types in philosophy, see C. D. Broad, *Five Types of Ethical Theory*, London: Routledge, 1930 or S. C. Pepper, *World Hypotheses*, 5th ed. Univ. Calif. Press, 1966.

But it is not easy to keep this distinction between classes and types. Often types are used as classes, and we begin to classify ourselves by means of types, thereby severing our fluid natures into well-defined and mutually exclusive parts. To use a type concept as a class concept has crippling results.

Also for the body-politic: when we use types as classes, they become literal stereotypes and work in a procrustean manner. A typical German or a typical American brings a typical image to mind, and this image has nothing to do with the legal definition of nationality. But should the typical be implemented by the national, that is, should the typical image become the class definition for the national, then all German and American nationals must conform to a stereotypical image, resulting in political exclusion and even genocide.

We tend to speak of types wherever we try to combine wide general principles together with single particular instances. Then types help to organize a vast number of similar events into rough groupings. (But the events must show similarity — and we shall come back to that). Vast numbers of events are hard to work with. For example, in the 1930's Gordon Allport and Henry Odbert at the Harvard Psychological Laboratory[7] compiled a list of 17,953 trait-names in English applicable to human personality, about as many different words as in all of Shakespeare, as in Joyce — descriptive terms such as: alert, aloof, alone, alcoholic, altruistic, alluring, altered, alive, all-round, almighty, etc. and etc., to 18,000. This list reveals the immense vocabulary at our disposal in only one tongue for describing human nature. If we are nominalists, these names of traits have no substantial existence or necessary connection to "personality" which is another such insubstantial word. But if we are even moderately realists, then these names might point beyond their verbal nature and might indicate something about the subtleties of human being. As Allport and Odbert say: "Each single term specifies in some way a form of human behavior" (p. vi). And these terms may point to a correspondence be-

---

[7] G. W. Allport & H. S. Odbert, "Trait-Names: A Psycho-lexical Study", *Psycholog. Monographs, Psychological Review* XLVII:1, No. 211, 1936.

tween linguistic richness and psychological richness, and that perhaps (p.2) "a correspondence between linguistic convention and psychological truth [may be] very close".

If rich language and rich insight do bear on each other, then here already is one of the reasons for our falling off in psychological acuity, compared with just fifty years ago. We no longer allow ourselves to use naive language of the old days; much of the words regularly used for character perception are old hat or taboo: ethnic-racial words (Jew, Turk, Okie, Prussian), Biblical words for character (Jeremiah, Ruth, John); class words (blue-blood, servant class, street-urchin, pickaninny, bastard). The new 'Ologies' insist that such terms are prejudices and stereotypes, which do not help seeing but block it. The 'Ologies' have substituted another objectified language instead. So now we say "Fascist", "neurotic", "overcompensated", "overweight", "underdeveloped", "under-achiever", "elitist", "unrelated", "chauvinist"; and our perception by means of obscene epithets has moved from a landscape of low race, birth and region to a landscape of the low body.

But what can we do, unless we are Shakespeare or Joyce, with 18,000 trait names for understanding personality? The problem confronted by psychology-as-science is similar to that which confronts the sciences of nature which have before them one million species of animals or a quarter of a million kinds of plants.

So, psychologists, on the model of natural scientists, attempt to order the vast array into smaller groupings. Cattell, ten years after the Harvard study, reduced the 18,000 trait-names to 171 adjectives in twelve groups.[8] Another psychologist, Orth, once named 1500 sorts of feelings. But Thomas Aquinas, Descartes, and many moderns who think the same way, have reduced the panoply of feelings to eleven, or eight, or six, five, or just two basic types of emotion of which all others are composed. Clearly, the simplification of words aids the

---

[8] Cf. F. Gendre & C. Ogay, "L'évaluation de la personnalité à l'aide de l'Adjective Check List (ACL) de H. Gough", *Rev. Suisse de Psychol.* 32/4, 1973, pp. 332–33.

reduction to types. You will notice here that we have entered into a numerical kind of thinking. We have assumed the scientistic eye that sees by means of numbers. Specific qualities, each with its trait-names, are viewed as a mass of chaotic quantity calling for ordering by reduction into a few types, as if the less the variety, the more that we know.

In short, type concepts fill a particular place in the ordering of events. They serve as intermediaries between a variegated world of huge quantities of bare particulars and the abstract world of general principles and classes — and types partake of both worlds.[9] They are both *anschaulich*, descriptive, as well as abstract, conceptual. By connecting individual and universal, or Variety and Oneness, they solve the problem of this Tagung, and we could sit down here. But there is more.

One question besetting type theory is this: Are types mental constructs that we impose on the world or are types given with the world? Are they artificial or natural? Have they a logical-epistemological status or an ontological one? When I call you an extraverted feeling type is this a way of organizing perceptions of you, or am I saying something essential about your nature that is given with it?

Some biologists insist that types are natural groups and that one cannot help but speak of types in the life sciences because they are empirically evident — right before the eyeball as are the shapes of animals. Types do not have to be constructed; they simply can be observed. For 370 million years and in a variety of more than 800,000 sorts, there is a creature divided into head with antennae, 3 pairs of mandibles, a thorax with three pairs of legs, often wings, and an abdomen. This type or "Bauplan" is an insect and a morphe of creepy-crawly life right there, not a Platonic idea or an ideal artifice, or a nominalistic construction. It is a visible fact of a tangible world.[10]

---

[9] Both Goethe and Dilthey, if in different ways, made the connection between universal and particular to be the essential characteristic of the type concept and thus the essence of their type theories. Cf. Koort, pp. 193–95.

[10] From Schindewolf, p. 15; cf. Marjorie Grene, "On the Nature of Natural Necessity" in her *The Understanding of Nature*, Dordrecht/Boston: Reidel, 1974, p. 236: "the very subject matter of biology... demands a reference to standards, types or norms...".

But in psychology, types are not empirically visible. I may *see* coarse blonde-hair, set jaw, and skilful hands, but I can only *infer* courage or determination. Physical anthropology — measurements of human bodies — gives only the grossest sort of information about the psyche of those bodies.[11]

Because psychological types are not directly observable, it has been a major exercise of personality research to make them more visible.[12] Experiments demonstrate or test singled-out factors of personality: cognitive abilities such as reading speed, syllogistic reasoning, word-fluency; or motor abilities such as aiming, reaction time, manual dexterity. This is what most experimental psychologists of personality, are busy with. Then these low-level multiple factors can be computed and integrated into second-and third-level groupings called intelligence, reasoning, creativity, and then, finally, high-level types of personality may be empirically verified as clusters of these trait factors. Then a type has some demonstrability. "True to type" means predictable reactions. Then a term like *introvert* becomes operational and a piece of positive knowledge.[13]

---

[11] Constitutional typologies (Pavlov, Kretschmer, and others reviewed by Lessa), including the one of left/right brain hemispheres, cannot escape the more fundamental problem of the psyche/soma pairing. As Lessa points out, constitutional typologies are least problematic in areas of biological pathologies, and most questionable when they formulate sociological (criminality — Lombroso; race; class) or psychological differences. Teplov (*op. cit. inf,* p. 4) points to the difficulties of directly relating types of nervous systems with types of behaviors — a fundamental critique of Pavlov's theory. See further A. Portmann, *Don Quijote und Sancho Pansa,* Basel: Reinhardt, 1964. Another sort of psyche/soma correlation is implied by Lavater's physiognomic view (see below) who conceives the connection between physique and character to be *imagistic* rather than literal.

[12] "No elements of personality are observable with perfect directness; all are inferred from behavioral indexes", N. Sanford, "Personality: Its Place in Psychology", in S. Koch, ed., *Psychology. A Study of a Science* Vol. 5, N.Y.: McGraw Hill, 1963, p. 514. The task of making personality observable is treated thoroughly in J. R. Royce, ed., *Multivariate Analysis and Psychological Theory,* London/N.Y.: Academic Press, 1973.

[13] The deepest problem in this method of establishing "high-level" types through "low-level" demonstration of traits lies not where we might suppose: the disjunction between the levels. (Empirical research, [Royce, ed.] continues to complain of an inverse proportion between high-level integrative ideas such as types backed

The chief urge behind the attempts to devise tests for Jung's eight types (Grey-Wheelwright, Myers-Briggs) has been to establish them as observable 'facts' acceptable to 'science'. In the great corpus of Jung's work his types offer the best place for the succubus of the science fantasy to latch, or leech, on.

Empirical psychology approaches uniqueness in the same manner. Uniqueness is a CPID, a "consistent pattern of individual difference". One must first chart consistencies before one can begin to see what is different. It begins with sames to find differents; groups to find singles; egalities to find oddities. The unique becomes the atypical, abnormal, deviate — an approach which we took up here two years ago. This approach separates human uniqueness from human sameness, missing that they are interchangeable perspectives and not literal actualities. At one moment I can view any aspect of myself as common, a moment later as unique. My very oddness that splits me from humankind can become, in a shift of vision, the common bond that joins me with others. The soul in Platonic usage is always both an all-soul, an *anima mundi*, and an individualization.

The vampiric metaphor I just used is apt for what goes on in typing. In the move to establish a type from a number of personal traits, the traits themselves are sucked out and drained into the larger factors. Actual concrete qualities of personality lose their blood to attitudes and functions. This happens every day when we look at ourselves typologically.

---

with few 'facts' and low-level empirical regularities demonstrated by immense data — suggesting an epistemological disjunction between ideal types and empirical traits.) Rather the problem rests on a fundamental fallacy: the assumption that the low-level concepts are 'closer to facts' and directly observable while high-level concepts such as "introvert" are theoretical and indirectly inferred. This assumption has been soundly rebuked by B. D. Mackenzie & S. L. MacKenzie "A Revised Systematic Approach to the History of Psychology", *J. Hist. Behav. Sci*, 10, 1974, p. 338: no matter at what 'level' we operate, we are working with concepts. As Sir Cyril Burt put it: "The theory of the concept is prior to the operation for measuring the concept", *Brit. J. Statis. Psychol.* 11, 1958, p. 57. The problem of conceptualization of *person* and *personality* in relation to measurement is examined carefully in the papers by Fiske and by Sells in Royce (ed.).

Let us say that I have good thinking and poor feeling. Yet, there are specific traits of thinking which I cannot perform — keeping my checkbook accurately, understanding the principles of information theory, or *Mengenlehre*, or symbolic logic, or how the television can be repaired; I may still stumble over the correct grammar of 'that' and 'which' in clauses, daylight-saving-time or Celsius-Fahrenheit conversions. These may each be miserable inferiorities in my thinking, even though I can perform many other analytical, logical, and systematic activities with precision, speed, and ease. Similarly, there are specific qualities in my supposedly poor feeling function that not only do not conflict with thinking but enhance it, such as feeling the value of a first-rate idea and subtly and aesthetically differentiating it from a second-rate one, or experiencing the ethical consequences of trains of thought or organizational planning. As well, despite this poor feeling function I may nonetheless be a loyal friend, a magnanimous host, a charitable critic of my students, admit and inwardly contain my despairs, and not be afraid to call a spade a spade in behalf of my values. In other words, particular moral and characterological, and even technical proficiencies, are altogether drained off into typological notions. A type consists in traits. Because usually a type is defined as the axial system that holds traits together or simply as their principle of correlation, it has no substance of its own. Its substance is in the traits. To let go the multiplicity and exquisite variety of the 18,000 traits is to lose the stuff and gut of persons and turn them into types.

The emptiness of types, the hollowness implied by the very word, their 'invisibility', causes another problem. As Koort[14] has observed, whenever we talk of types we soon begin talking of examples and cases. Types call for living instances. Jung's book needs its Chapter X to make visible images with anecdotes and persons so that we can imagine all that has gone before. This peculiar process of thought — the need for examples — casts a shadow over all uses of typological thinking, especially in psychology and psychiatry. Is there not the danger of filling in the empty notion with concrete persons, creating

---

[14] Koort, p. 255f.

cases even in the pathological sense to fill in our typical forms of pathology.

Pavlov's typology requires four types of reactions of higher nervous systems. But empirically only two dogs could be found to fit the phlegmatic type — and since his time, none.[15] One empirical study of Jung's types finds only five of the eight. The study does not question the system, the eight; it questions only its own method which didn't find the full array of examples.[16] In other words, once we have begun to think in types, we have to see examples, or find them, or invent them. We use the empirical to fill the ideal. When we cast persons into these kinds of being, severe ontological consequences follow.

Another consequent is that types tend to be set up as typologies, as systems. Jasper's typology (1919) aims, as does Jung's, to grasp the "basic positions of the psyche and the forces which move it".[17] But to do this, he must have system (three main forms, three subforms, and then three further subforms of each of these). He defends this method on the grounds that only systematic schema can provide comprehensive theory (p. 17). When types want to be comprehensive — and unless they do they offer no necessity and have little explanatory or ordering power — then, as McKinney[18] shows by analyzing typologies, they tend to become bi-polar, set in oppositions. Even a typology of type theories bi-polarizes them as empirical *versus* ideal, epistemological *versus* ontological, structural *versus* correlational,[19] bi-polar *versus* triadic.

We may speak of them fluidly, as moving along a register between less and more, but their construction and their language remains dyadic. Tests that would type us always ask dyadic questions: do you prefer to enter buildings with large doorways or small; do you prefer

---

[15] Teplov, in Grey (ed.), p. 114–5.

[16] L. Gorlow, N. R. Simonson & H. Krauss, "An Empirical Investigation of the Jungian Topology", *Brit. J. Soc. Clin. Psychol.* 5, 1966, pp. 108–17.

[17] K. Jaspers, "Vorwort", *Psychologie der Weltanschauungen*, Berlin: Springer, 1919.

[18] J. C. McKinney, "The Polar Variables of Type Construction", *Social Forces* (Baltimore) 35:4, 1957, pp. 300–06; Hempel & Oppenheim, p. 78.

[19] Cf. Hempel & Oppenheim, p. 4.

red flowers or blue, women with large buttocks or large breasts. Test literature over and again uses the word *versus*,[20] creating a world for an ego to choose between events that hitherto had not seemed opposed or to demand preferences. We understand introversion only as less or moving away from, or versus extraversion, thinking only as less, or moving away from, or versus feeling. Soon, the contrasting poles of *one and the same thing on the same dimension* have become polar oppositions, then contradictions: to think is not to feel; to sense is not to intuit. (Contradiction is of course not necessary to type construction, but we are not all 'thinking types' who can handle logic, especially not when assessing ourselves and others.) So the polarisation of type construction polarizes us; we feel *either* introverted *or* extraverted. The inferior then becomes the other pole, a cut-off impossibility, or a heroic task to be developed through "sacrifice of the superior function".

These polarities also make us lose the *images* of feeling, or intuition, or extraversion, as states in themselves. We see them only dynamically in tension with an opposite. But in actual life, a "feeler" — who can be depicted in literature or biography, or as a hysteric or depressive syndrome with a host of idiosyncratic traits, or depicted as a child of Luna, or Venus, or Saturn — can well be presented without any polarity or opposition. Planetary types, the thirty character epitomes of Theophrastus, and the syndromes of psychopathology as reaction types do not have to be set up in polar systems. Imaginative, depicted types as backgrounds differ from systematic typologies. I would even hazard that systematic typologies are fundamentally anti-imaginal and that the fantasy of types disturbs our appreciation of the image and our ability to imagine.

Here I have myself set up a polarity between imagining and typing, and soon we could be arguing that the more we perceive in typologies,

---

[20] E.g., P. E. Vernon, "Multivariate Approaches to the Study of Cognitive Styles", in *Multivariate Analysis and Psychological Theory* (J. R. Royce, ed.), London/N.Y.: Academic Press, 1973, pp. 128–34, a thorough review of contemporary typology scales presented throughout in terms of *"versus"*.

the less we do so in images, and eventually they could become contra-
dictories: to imagine is not to type, to type is not to imagine.

We may circumvent this danger when we remember that typological
polarities are themselves an image: an image of a sliding scale along
a straight line. Statements about ourselves in terms of bi-polar types
present fantasies of "where we are placing ourselves" lineally. I locate
myself on an axis which offers only two possibilities, more or less,
with gradations of advancement or retreat from the goal values of this
axis.

Now, 'advancement' and 'retreat' belong to heroic imagery, so it is
not surprising that personality assessments of types usually rely on
ego-introspection, ("self-reports" through preference questions), and
that Jung's four types are conceived as functions of ego-consciousness.[21]

This brings us to the relation of type and image — a subject with
a long history which shows types presenting themselves as images. For
example, poetic types are persons from literary legends used as *uni-
versali fantastici* by Vico. Planetary types are figures of Gods displayed
in the images of myths. Biblical types are persons of the Old Testament
seen as *vor-bilder* of the New. Morphological types are figures in
nature seen, in different ways by Goethe, Cuvier, and Whewill, as
manifestations of *Urbilder*.[22] Goethe's deep insight into the type
concept was that the type is *immediately presented in the image*. A type
cannot be separated from the image in which it appears. We see types
by seeing images; or rather, when we see a type, actually we are seeing
an image. No longer is it a matter of the difference between types and
images as objects of perception. Now it becomes a matter of viewing
one and the same event by typing it or by imagining it, either by means
of the perspective of types or that of images. This conjunction of type

---

[21] The association of the functions with ego-consciousness comes out clearly in
the 'heroic' description Jung gives of a "differentiated" function: it can be recog-
nized by its "strength, stability, consistency, reliability, and adaptedness", whereas
an inferior function is quite 'unheroic': "lack of self-sufficiency and consequent
dependence on people and circumstances... disposing us to moods and crotcheti-
ness... suggestible and labile" (§ 956).

[22] Cf. Koort, pp. 43–90 & 119–28.

and image implies also that images are not romantically free of typicalities and predictabilities.

We have come to a new place. Now types are not opposed to images, but are a special way of imaging. Rather than conceiving images typically and organizing our styles of perception into types, we are beginning to see types and their systems imaginally. Now by imagining a type in our minds, instantly the type moves into images that display it. Instead of our having to multiply instances to prove the type, the type multiplies images out of itself. Now a typical introvert is not conceptually defined or described, as a cluster of traits. It is my younger brother sunk in thought on the beach under seagulls; myself blushing last night when introduced to the Chairman's sleek, lithe daughter. Types have now become empty casting molds, out of which a pattern of images flows, and the mind, by generating examples, moves from type to image.

When this move of the mind is put into Biblical typology, then Old Testament figures are literal prefigurations of New Testament historical fulfillments.[23] When this move from type to image is put into animal types (Whewill), then a type is manifested in the varieties of itself in living images and we can reconstruct the prehistoric *Urtier*, the genotype, from these phenomenal images. The power of a type to image itself on, its procession in images, is taken by Biblical, literary, or biological typology, as a literal movement in the world of history, as an emanation from archetypes into images. Then we try to recompose or 'verify' a type — or an archetype — by collecting instances. We do not need to think in this manner.

All we need do is recognize that when we are seeing types we have begun to imagine in a figurational mode. We have begun to personify. We have begun to envision presences as the determining powers. And, that life is a fulfillment of their predictions. Things run true-to-type in that each thing fulfills its image, imagines itself typically into itself, each image held within the relief of its specific form. It is the typicality

---

[23] Cf. J. A. Galdon, *Typology and Seventeeth-Century Literature*, The Hague: Mouton, 1975, esp. Chaps. II–IV.

inherent to the image that we acknowledge in science by speaking of prediction and in psychology by speaking of the archetypal. It is this typicality in an image that sets its limit and suggests its placing (*topos*).

So the evidence for a type is in the vision that sees its images. The word *evidence* refers to an act of *vision*. Seeing types is a Platonic act which cannot be established by an Aristotelian method. Two eyes, even with microscope, can not equal that third eye. To restore images to types means seeing types as a mode of imaging which cannot be satisfied by empirically gathered evidence. (It is anyway the type in our eye — the ability to see similarities and to compare — that allows us to see resemblances in what we gather for evidence and in the questionnaires that yield this evidence.) The scientistic search for evidence betrays itself for what it is: loss of morphic vision, an eye unopened to the image.

Jung's Typology: Let us turn now to Jung's types, focussing on only a few considerations. (All quotations are from Volume 6 of the *Collected Works* unless otherwise indicated.)

First of all, his types are formed into a polar construction such as we discussed. The polar construction makes the types not mere random eclectic categories, but a *typology*. It is this system which gives them their high-level explanatory power. They are axiomatically connected with one another in a tightly-knit, tension-filled "cross" (§ 983). This cross is also all-inclusive. Jung claims completeness for his typology (§ 843; *CW 11*, § 246), much as does Aristotle for his four causes, Schopenhauer for his four principles of reason, Popper for his four root metaphors, Pavlov for his four types of nervous systems, Russell for his four types of philosophical statements.[24] The claim to comple-

---

[24] Cf. B. M Teplov "Problems in the Study of General Types of Higher Nervous Activity in Man and Animals" in J. A. Gray (ed.) *Pavlov's Typology*, Oxford: Pergamon, 1964, p. 113. The types of philosophical statements in Russell and Wittgenstein are discussed by K. R. Popper, *Conjectures and Refutations*, 3rd. ed., London: Routledge 1969, pp. 69–70. (In both Pavlov and Russell/Wittgenstein the 'fourth' type gives difficulties, or seems of another kind than the other three.) I have discussed the metaphor of the four-fold root as it appears in Aristotle's Causes, Schopenhauer, etc. in my *Emotion* (London, Routledge, p. 18–21,1960) p 246–48.

teness seems characteristic of four-fold systems. That is, it belongs to the rhetoric of the archetypal perspective of fourness to present itself as a systematic whole, a mandala with an internal logic by means of which the system defends itself as all-encompassing.[25]

Because Jung's types are laid out axiomatically as a polar construction, the types rest on their 'Ology', on principles even more fundamental than the types themselves: the principles of opposition,[26] even mutual exclusion, operating between the pairs of "subject and object", "inner and outer", "conscious and unconscious", "rational and irrational", "superior and inferior", "mind and heart", "actual and possible". Anyone using the types in their systematic form is immediately implicated in the premises — and problems — on which the system depends. Jung's typology, presented modestly as a description of empirical functions and attitudes, nonetheless implicates an entire *Weltbild* of oppositions and energies held together by its mandala form. If not overtly an ontology or metaphysics, at least we cannot escape its *Weltanschauung*. It is set forth as the basic structure of our consciousness.

The connection between typology and mandala is also biographical. Both appeared immediately after Jung's "creative breakdown" (Ellenberger), euphemistically termed his "fallow period" by the Editors of the *Collected Works* (p. v) but what Jung himself calls his "confrontation with the unconscious" (1913–1919 ca.). Typology and mandala both serve the same purpose of ordering irreconcilable conflicts. Jung had written on types before his years of self-analysis, but the final formulation as an eight- or sixteen-pointed conceptual mandala came only after this period (published 1921). Functionally, the interlocking system of the typology and its power of explaining one's differences within oneself and the world, as well as one's differences

---

[25] The system is envisioned *spatially*, wholly in terms of the subject/object relation. Others have tried to give the typology a *temporal* dimension, e.g. H. Mann, M. Siegler., H. Osmond, "The Many Worlds of Time", *J. Analyt. Psychol.* 13, 1968, pp. 33–56.

[26] The relation between the kinds of oppositions in Jung is discussed in my long note 101, *Eranos 42–1973*, p. 303.

with the world and one's enemies (Freud and Adler as ostensible effici-
ent cause of the book), serve, as does any good system, as an apotropaic or paranoic buttress of egoconsciousness (to which Jung attributes
the types) against what he called Dionysian dissolution.

We still turn to typology when we need system. When our ego-
comprehension is disoriented and anxious, then we turn to astrology,
typology, archetypology, and the like. Types still bring with them their
origins in defense against confusions by means of systems. Appeals to
founding Jung's psychology scientifically upon types (Meier) and to
relying more on them for understanding clinical psychodynamics
(Fordham) bear the same witness to apotropaic system-building for
the unpredictabilities of the "confrontation with the unconscious" and
its images.

Our moves in psychology recapitulate Jung's moves. Ideas have
roots in the necessities of our abnormal psychologies — in Jung's no
less than ours. That is why it is so important to understand the internal necessity of his ideas in connection with his psyche, for one and
the same psychic process continues in our own work when we use his
ideas. They bring with them their roots. When we turn to typology,
we need to see when Jung turned, and that he so rarely turned there
again as he deepened his work from types to archetypes. Moreover,
unlike Meier and Fordham, Jung had no need to establish his types
with scientific or clinical literalism which would turn modes of seeing
into things seen.[27]

Despite their mandala structure, Jung does not give his types archetypal significance as such. They are not presented as *Idealbilder, Urty-
pen,* or *Urformen.* Only the four-fold system is archetypal, not the
types.

---

[27] Jung's intention with his types was neither scientific nor clinical but Kantian
(pp. xiv–xv). Kant is often referred to in this book, e.g. §512, even as an allegory
for the superior function opposed to Dionysus for the inferior (§§908–10). The
Kantian fantasy of the typology thus correlates with the 'Dionysian' experiences
preceding it (1913–1919). On the four-fold mandala as defense against the dissolution of Dionysus-Wotan-Nietzsche, see my "Dionysus in Jung's Writings" *Spring
1972,* pp. 191–205. On Jung and Kant, see J. R. Heisig's collection of passages in
his *Imago Dei in C. G. Jung,* Bucknell Univ. Press, forthcoming.

A closer look at the way Jung speaks of the types, however, suggests that they too are archetypal. For what determines type? Here the a priori element enters: Jung speaks of a "numinal accent" falling on one type or another (§ 982). This selective factor determining type is unaccounted for. It is simply given. A numinal accent selects our bias toward what becomes our superior function which drives the others into the background (§ 984). We begin to see that the four types are more than mere manners of functioning. There is something more at work in them, something numinal — and "numinal" means "divine". And surely when in the grips of our typical set, as we cannot help but be when we imagine ourselves typologically, the structuring power of the type is like that of an archetype or mythologem. Especially the experience of the inferior function, also referred to as numinous, brings with it a radical shift of perspective, as if there has been an ontological shift, an initiation into a new cosmos or archetypal *seinsweise*.

An archetypal background for the four functions has already been intimated by Jung himself. He speaks of a philosophical typology in Gnosticism or Hellenistic syncretism (§§ 14, 964) by means of which human beings could be called *hylikoi*, *psychikoi*, or *pneumatikoi*. Jung does not document this typology but Professor Sambursky considers that these terms were applied less to actual persons than to the imaginal persons of Neoplatonism, especially by Plotinus. These imaginal regions and their beings might thus be the archetypal imagination at work in the functions, giving to them each its numinal accent and each its ontological significance as structuring ground of consciousness.

Then *hylikoi*, or *physis*, with its attendant ideas of matter, body, actual physical reality would be the archetypal principle in what Jung called sensation; *psychikoi*, or soul, with its attendant Jungian description of love, value, experience, relatedness, woman, salt, colour would be the archetype within and behind what Jung called feeling; *pneumatikoi*, or spirit, with its attendant descriptions in terms of light, vision, swiftness, invisibilities, timelessness, would be what Jung called intuition; and finally, not expressly distinguished in this Hellenistic triad, *nous*, *logos*, or *intellectus*, with its capacity for order and cognitive intelligence, would be the archetypal principle that Jung called the thinking function. (Jung himself identifies thinking with *pneumatikoi*, § 14.)

This archetypal background gives a deeper sense to what Jung says about the four functions. For instance, if sensation so often brings with it an uncomfortable inferiority, and intuition, superiority, the reason is not functional, but archetypal — the one being hylitic and bearing all the aspersions put upon physis in our tradition, the other, pneumatic, windy with the idealizations of the spirit.[28] Or, it is hardly a feeling function, as an ego-disposable mode of adaptation through evaluations, which can support such redemptive features that Jung claims for "feeling" (cf. *CW 14*, §§ 328–34; *CW 16*, §§ 488–91; *CW 13*, § 222, and also *CW 8*, §§ 668–69 where his discussion of evidence for soul turns on "feelings"), unless we realize that "feeling" has become a secular psychologism for soul.[29]

Furthermore, we now can grasp better that connection which Jung makes between the four functions and the wholeness of the "total personality" (*CW 14*, § 261), or Adam (ibid. §§ 555–57). For now we would be dealing with the root archetypal structures or cosmoi of Western human being, our four "natures" as Jung calls them (*CW 14*, §§ 261, 265; cf. *CW 11*, §§ 184–85) which as he says there in *Mysterium Coniunctionis*, are an archetypal prefiguration of "what we today call the schema of functions". The four types are thus not mere empirical

---

[28] Practitioners' descriptions of the puer psychology of young men often call them "intuitive" and airy, needing "sensation" and earth. The older language of elemental natures has been unwittingly associated with that of functional types. Actually, the practitioner is discerning young *pneumatikoi* whose archetypal basis in spirit cannot be reduced to an over-developed empirical ego-function of intuition.

[29] Willeford, "The Primacy of Feeling", *J. Analyt. Psychol.* 21, 1976, pp. 115–133 argues for a special place for the feeling function beyond Jung's polar equalities. Because Willeford takes feeling to be *the* function of the "subjective sphere" (an idea which brings us again to Jung's early identification of feeling with introversion) he is suggesting that its relation with soul is different and more important than that of the other functions.

functions. They are the physical, spiritual, noetic, and psychic cosmoi in which man moves and imagines.[30]

The ancients placed these cosmoi one on top of the other and fantasied the ideal man moving through them from below to above. Jung too imagines the individuating person moving through the functions, not ascensionally in his model, yet still redemptively from one-sidedness to four-foldedness. Although these archetypal powers of the ancients present themselves conceptually, they are nonetheless archetypal persons of the imaginal to begin with.

By this I do not mean to replace intuition with spirit, and feeling with psyche, etc., or to equate them or reduce them. Rather I am maintaining that the functions have been carrying archetypal projections which gives them, and typology, a numinal accent. Types conceal archetypes. The contemporary cult of feeling, for instance, is a disguised psychologistic substitution for cult of *soul*. The frequent attack on *intellect* (metaphysics and theology) through Jung's writings and letters has resulted in poor critical thinking in the Jungian school because the archetypal principle within thinking has been devalued. Unless we recognize the imaginal persons in our personal modes of functioning these modes lose their numinal accent. Only an archetypal appreciation of the functions can take them out of the hands of the ego. Unless the great root principles of Western man's orientation are seen for what they are, as the modes in which the imaginal operates (functions) in all realms of being, they, and we, are condemned to psychological jargon without numinal accent. Thus we must cling to the types for orientation since they do conceal the archetypal natures of our Western compass.

Jung did not intend his typology to be used for typing persons.

---

[30] That Jung did not elaborate the archetypal aspect of the four functions has given rise to many attempts to deal with this hiatus by means of correlations with various sorts of cosmic constants: humours, elements, geometric forms, zodiacal signs, principles such as Love, Truth, Beauty, and Light, alchemical substances (salt, sulphur, mercury, and lead or a composite tetrasome of four metals), alchemical colors, or even the eight world religions (A. Toynbee, *An Historian's Approach to Religion*, Oxford Univ. Press, 1956, p. 138).

Precisely the way in which his types are used and experimented with in the Grey-Wheelwright and Briggs-Myers tests — the clinical scientism — is what Jung expressly did not intend. He writes:

> "It is not the purpose of a psychological typology to classify human beings into categories — this in itself would be pretty pointless" (§986).

> "Far too many readers have succumbed to the error of thinking that Chapter X ('General Description of the Types') represents the essential content and purpose of the book, in the sense that it provides a system of classification and a practical guide to a good judgement of human character... This regrettable misunderstanding completely ignores the fact that this kind of classification is nothing but a childish parlour game... My typology... [is not meant] to stick labels on people at first sight. It is not a physiognomy... For this reason I have placed the general typology... at the end of the book... I would therefore recommend the reader... to immerse himself first of all in chapters II and V. He will gain more from them than from any typological terminology superficially picked up, since this serves no other purpose than a totally useless desire to stick on labels" (pp. xiv–xv.).

What then was the "fundamental tendency" of the book if it was not to type persons? Jung sets it out most clearly:

> "Its purpose is rather to provide a critical psychology... First and foremost, it is a critical tool for the research worker" (§986). "The typological system I have proposed is an attempt... to provide an explanatory basis and theoretical framework for the boundless diversity... in the formation of psychological concepts" (§987).

Note that: not diversity of *human beings,* but diversity of *psychological concepts.* As a critical psychology, a psychology that offers a critical tool for examining ideas, it belongs to epistemology, and it was a necessary consequent of Jung's placing psyche first. As Aniela Jaffé has said here at Eranos 1971 — referring to that period between 1913 and 1919 when Jung had been convinced through his own experience of the primacy of psychic reality — "the soul cannot be the object of judgement and knowledge, but judgement and knowledge are the object of the soul". The types were to provide the fundamental psychological antinomies which enter into every judgement in psychology. The typology was intended as a means of seeing through statements about the soul.[31] It was an attempt at a differentiated understanding of the variety of human psychologies (§§ 851–53).

The consequence of using a multiple tool is psychological relativism. This Jung knew; and it is even a corollary purpose of this *Types* to see through and relativize any psychological position. He says in the Epilogue to that work:

> "...in the case of psychological theories the necessity of a plurality of explanations is given from the start"... "an intellectual understanding of the psychic process must end in paradox and relativity"(§§855–56; cf. 846–49).

Though intended as a Kantian critical tool for research and imagined as a "trigonometric net" or "crystallographic axial system" (§ 986) of structural principles behind personal viewpoints, the personal creeps in the back door of this the least imagistic of all his major later works, as if the shadow of the book is its Chapter Ten. There the eight types are depicted anecdotally, imagistically.

And here we all get caught by his book — not for the superb analysis of the mediaeval universals problem, or his examinations of Schiller and Spitteler, Jordan and James, for how few even read this part of the work! — no, we all fall for these descriptions (of the introverted intuitive type, the extraverted sensation type, etc.) and take them literally as empirical persons. Such is the movement of the psyche when reading the book: it moves from the abstract to the *anschaulich*. Types become images. In the hollow roughedged space the psyche would have an engraved gem-stone, a little depiction of a personified image. The evidence that the psyche desires is not satisfied empirically, for it seeks an image: an anecdote, a Theophrastian character, a psychiatric case, a 'typical example' from life or literature, a Saint, an ikon of visible traits that acounts for the numinal accent of my type. Without these personified images to give precise substance to a type, a type more easily rigidifies into a defined class.

---

[31] For a use of Jung's typology as he intended it (the examination of psychological *ideas* rather than persons), see B. Klopfer and J. M. Spiegelman, "Some Dimensions of Psychotherapy", *Speculum Psychologiae* (C. T. Frey, ed.) Zürich: Rascher, 1965.

Until the hollow of the type be specified with its image, it is our
own face we see in typologies. Don't we tend to turn to them most
when we are self-occupied, neurasthenic, narcisstically depressed?
When we need ego-support? Typologies fascinate and convince because they are methods of mirroring what we most look for — self-
perception, recognition of our individual image. And the more we
gain this insight into our uniqueness and present ourselves as an individual image, the less fascinating and convincing typology: we say,
"we no longer fit in". Our individual image has become shaped more
distinctly than the empty rough-edged form that reflects us each in its
equalizing measure.

And every well-written typology, such as those depictions in Chapter X or in the older psychiatry texts or in astrological *Characterkunde*,
will capture us and equalize us into its image — especially the pathologized image. As we journey through the planetary houses, typical
syndrome to syndrome, we become the description, embody the
diseases one by one, fit into each chapter. Such is the power of the
well-shaped image, and such is the suffering of the soul until it be
perceived in its own image. Thus within every typological system there
lurks the abstract emptiness in which we lose our uniqueness until we
have the sense of our own morphological individuality.

II. *Persons as Faces*

> "The world lives in order to develop the
> lines on its face."   T. E. Hulme[32]

C. G. Jung wrote: "Since individuality... is absolutely unique,
unpredictable, and uninterpretable... the therapist must abandon all
his preconceptions and techniques..." (*16*;§ 6). We have been attempting this, abandoning even one of the techniques, typing, derived from

---

[32] From "Cinders" in his *Speculations*, H. Read, ed., London: Kegan Paul,
1924, p. 229.

Jung. But our problem remains: how to perceive the human pheno-menon before us in its uninterpretable uniqueness?

Here we might turn from the empirical and scientistic to the more philosophical psychologies. We should expect help from phenomeno-logy whose very business is to confront the phenomenon directly, or from existentialism whose concern is mainly with the existential person, or from the psychoanalytic tradition whose focus of effort is the individual case in the privacy of practice.

But in the first case, phenomenology, "there is no person as such for Husserl, only an empirical and a transcendental ego, united tenously by the body and behaviour" as global abstractions, while Merleau-Ponty gives us hermeneutics, interpretative *meanings* of body and gesture across the board, in all of us, as universals. In the second case, existentialism, Sartre "dissolves personal encounter into a petrifying scotophilic *look* — a look which overlooks the crucial minutiae" which are unique and precisely that which govern one's existence; while Heidegger's concern is neither with the person nor with the particular except as modes of Dasein, and this despite all his appeal to the concrete. In the third case, psychoanalysis, Freud and his patient never looked each other in the face during the procedure of their ritual, and Lacan admits that: "A psychoanalysis normally proceeds to its termination without revealing to us very much of what our patient derives in his own right from his particular sensitivity to colors or calamities, from the quickness of his grasp of things or the urgency of his weaknesses of the flesh, from his power to retain or to invent — in short, from the vivacity of his tastes."[33] Again the nomothetic dominates. In philosophical psychologies,[34] as much as in scientistic

---

[33] I am indebted to E. S. Casey, Yale University, for the substance and quota-tions of this paragraph. (The Lacan passage is from his *Language of the Self*, p. 29.)

[34] "Typical psychological phenomena are what phenomenological psychologists have traditionally studied (von Kaam, Fischer, Lauffer, Cloonan, Stevick, Co-laizzi)." E. Keen, "Studying Unique Events", paper read at the Amer. Psychol. Assoc. Meetings, Chicago, 1975, p. 18. Keen's solution — a *dialectic* between typical and unique — falls prey to its own philosophical assumption: typical and unique, general and particular are valid categories and problematically opposed.

nomothetic — of a science of general of universal laws.

psychologies, the individual is crowded to the wall by the general. So we must try another approach altogether.

Is it possible that the person before us already gives us his individuality. Could it be that his invisible essence is stamped right in his visible presence? Each human being bearing the traits of his uniqueness stamped upon him — this ancient idea is the common ground of all systems of characterology. And characterology, the study of visible signs for discovering the invisible in human nature, is a trunk root of psychology.

The relation between physique and character — as Kretschmer was to call his work — as well as deriving predictabilities from this relation, occurs already among Babylonians. Physiognomic omina revealed fate. Physique was related to character by means of a "when/then" formula — the language of prophetic magic not so very different from the language of predictional science. "When his hair and his face is long, then his days are long, he will be poor."[35] There is no distinction between character and fate. A character statement derived from physique is also a prophecy. When a woman shows features good for bearing children, then she will bear many children. Or according to a man's build, "The man is sinful, he will be killed by a weapon."[36] Taking our cue from Jung, when we read a person or his soul's contents (dreams) in order to predict fate (marriage, travel, psychosis), we are moving away from uniqueness which is both uninterpretable and unpredictable. To see essence of character does not mean that we can predict what will happen to that character. That psychologist who "can look into the seeds of time, and say which grain will grow and which will not" is the witch, says Shakespeare (*Macbeth* I, 3).

Greek treatises on physiognomics — and here the main influence on us is the *Physiognomonica* attributed to Aristotle — distinguished between character and prophecy, between psychology proper and magical or scientific predictabilities. The basic principle of reading character through physical visibility is stated straight off: "Dispositions

---

[35] F. R. Kraus, "Die physiognomischen Omina der Babylonier", *Mitt. d. Vorderasiat.-Aegypt. Gesellsch.* 40:2, 1935 (Leipzig).

[36] Ibid., p. 12.

follow bodily characteristics" (805a), and immediately there follows an assumption presented as evidence: "There never was an animal with the form of one kind and the mental character of another: the soul and body appropriate to the same kind always go together, and this shows that a specific body involves a specific mental character".

Aristotle next summarizes three different ways of reading persons. We can see them in terms of animal analogies,[37] and of geography and race, and of facial display of emotions. We see a person as bird-like or horsefaced, and as Greek or Egyptian, and as displaying the universal signs of anger or erotic excitement. These same three ways of understanding the looks of our fellows have continued to inform our tradition of physiognomics from Aristotle or before until our own day of research on stereotypes in perception and sociology of race relations. Besides these main methods, this little treatise codified observations that still come quick to the tongue: "Inhabitants of the north being brave and coarsehaired, whilst southern peoples are cowardly and have soft hair" (806b).[38] Later, this sort of north/south division became one between blondes and brunettes. Physical anthropology around 1900, and Havelock Ellis as well, produced studies to show that blondes are more "positive, dynamic, driving, aggressive, domineering, impatient, active, quick, hopeful, speculative, changeable, and variety-loving".[39] Jaensch's T-type was to be found, he said, mainly among blondes. Darker persons were of another type showing "romantischen Bluteinschlag", he said.[40]

---

[37] Perception of persons by means of animal analogies is deep in our language of traits. This language was of course powerfully shaped in English by Shakespeare who has over 4000 allusions to animals in his plays. Falstaff, Caliban, Richard III, and Ajax have the highest scores for character descriptions in animal terms. Cf. Audrey Yoder, *Animal Analogy in Shakespeare's Character Portrayal* (N. Y.: King's Crown, Columbia Univ., 1947), for statistics and excellent bibliography on the tradition of animal analogies.

[38] Cf. my *Re-Visioning Psychology*, p. 259, nn. 112 & 113 for a psychological view of the north-south polarity.

[39] The material is presented and criticized in Lessa.

[40] E. R. Jaensch, *Grundformen menschlichen Seins*, Berlin: Elsner, 1929, p. 325.

Though the discrimination of persons according to ethnic, racial, and geographical notions is one of the oldest and most basic habits in the tradition of psychological assessment of persons, it is now fully suppressed. We do not dare discriminate along these lines. Even the term "discrimination" has taken on a pejorative 'elitist' sense. We no longer allow ourselves to discriminate differences by means of north and south, smooth and hairy, dark and light, oily and dry. Because we no longer dispose of a richly emotional language for insighting the historical and geographical shadow in the psyche, this entire metaphorical possibility becomes unconscious, returning as literal racial discrimination in the world. But *stereotypes are images*, modes of imagination that present physiognomies of the shadow, allowing me to see my own in contrast. By means of these ethnic epithets I am able to discriminate a region of differences between myself and others, and locate each psyche within a distinct landscape, giving it history and soil. Of course all communal thinking, all egalitarian 'Ologies' taboo as prejudices these modes of perceptive discrimination, forcing ethnic images and metaphors into literalisms that project shadow rather than letting see and feel shadow.

These stereotypical modes — animal, geographical, emotional — were part of the physiognomics by means of which the ancient world understood and described persons.[41] In ancient medicine or philosophy, drama or literature, rhetoric or biography (as the *imagines* of the Emperors by Suetonius), character could be differentiated by tell-tale signs explained by axioms collected in physiognomic handbooks.[42]

For instance, Emperor Julian was declared demonic by Gregory of Nazianzus[43] in terms that everyone could understand: one had only to look at the man: his unsteady neck, jerking shoulders, unstable feet,

---

[41] Cf. the superb monograph by Eliz. C. Evans, "Physiognomics in the Ancient World", *Trans. Amer. Philosoph. Soc.* 59:5, 1969.

[42] Evans, pp. 6–17 on the treatises and handbooks.

[43] Gregory of Nazianzus, *Or. 4, Contra Iulianum*, 1; *Or. 5, Contra Iulianum*, 2. Cf. Evans, pp. 74–80.

unrestrained laughter, effeminacy. None of these traits were proper to the ideal image of Christian physique, and therefore Julian could not be but demonic. Anatomy is destiny. Julian of course had his own physiognomer who found his same traits laudatory, and Julian wrote on this very subject himself, insisting to his portraitist: "paint me exactly as you saw me". His nature was revealed in his face. But our task is not judging Emperor Julian, but candidate Carter, or our candidates for training as analysts. Let us look at some other approaches, less antique, for seeing persons, not as types, but as faces.

Darwin: What we have just learned from the ancients is that there is indeed a mode of perceiving persons directly: the person is his self-presentation. And we have learned that it will not be altogether possible to follow Jung's fantasy of existential objectivity and abandon all preconceptions, since when we see persons we see faces, and certain preconceptions — animal, racial, emotional — seem given with the face itself. The weak chin, bull neck, low brow, and fleshy lip are themselves images; the very phrases echo metaphorically. There have been various attempts in psychology, and we shall now be reviewing several, to work out *the relation between person and image*. For instance, does a knitted brow always indicate worry and a downturned lip sadness? This sort of question occupied Darwin.

Darwin's study, *The Expression of the Emotions in Man and Animals* was published in 1872, a year after his *Descent of Man*, and was conceived as part of that book which had come out a year earlier. The work on expression brought further evidence for his thesis of mental continuity, or the evolution of the human from other animal species. Even the human face and its variegated expressions so characteristic of what we consider uniquely human and unique in each human, if not divine, has its phylogenetic roots.

Darwin scrutinized the faces of the mentally ill, works of art, higher animals, adults from various cultures, and infants and children. (He had begun keeping a journal of his observations on his own children in 1840, 32 years before publishing his findings.) Since then similar work on similar groups has confirmed Darwin.[44] Facial expression of anger, joy, surprise, sorrow, fear appear early in life. Learning is not required for this appearance. Research with the congenitally blind also supports Darwin's thesis that what we show in emotional physiognomics rests mainly on innate factors that do not require seeing other faces. Cross-cultural studies, which have included such isolated and pre-literate peoples as the Fore and Dani of New Guinea, conclude: "The same facial expressions are associated with the same emotions, regardless of culture or language".[45] Darwin further suggested that physiognomy of any face was itself largely the result of emotional attitudes. Repeated emotional experiences lead to the development of permanent facial form (wrinkles, colouring, muscle tensions).

One does not have to accept Darwin's evolutional explanation even while we may accept both the innate expressive *analogies* between human and animal physiognomy and the innate *commonality* in all human faces as one more place where what Jung calls the "collective unconscious" manifests itself. The image that we present in our *Selbstdarstellung* — to use the term of Adolf Portmann — is the visibility of our emotional nature. Our surface presents our depth.

Szondi: Our next approach runs through Zürich. Type and image come together in the *Schicksalsanalyse* of Leopold (Lipot) Szondi. Briefly, Szondi is a Hungarian psychiatrist who lives and has his Institute in Zürich. He developed a diagnostic test and a therapeutic direction based upon discovering one's type through selecting among 48 radically pathologized images. One is shown photographs of the faces of paroxysmal epileptics, catatonic schizophrenics, criminal sadists, severe depressives — eight types in all — that have been culled from

---

[44] Paul Ekman (ed.), *Darwin and Facial Expression*: *A Century of Research in Review* (N. Y.: Academic Press, 1973).
    [45] Ekman, p. 219.

the brilliantly precise, descriptive psychiatry texts[46] of the early part of this century, when this sort of medical freak show was the delight of the adolescent, doing more, I suspect, for his education into the profundities of the psyche than the pornographic substitutes of today.

It is Szondi's theory that the genetic pattern shows in the face: the faces in the test are the extremist, purest visibilities of basic genetic types. Therefore, should I choose manic faces as more sympathetic, and catatonic faces as most repulsive, my selection derives — so he says — from my recessive genes working through my unconscious sympathies and antipathies. It is assumed that the person whose face I have chosen suffers from the specific type of psychiatric disorder which is potentially present in me owing to my recessive genes. These recessive genes rule the unconscious, forcing us to choose our partners, our professions, our sicknesses, and our deaths. By choosing a specific pathological physiognomy, we discover which specific type of personified monster is unconsciously affecting our *Schicksal* (destiny).

Before Szondi, already in 1878, Francis Galton,[47] Darwin's half-cousin and also an extraordinary person in the history of psychology, had begun making composite photographs of criminal and disease types, and of family members, by superimposing one exposure on another until he got the image of a face which brought out what he called hereditary traits. By an empirical technique he arrived at a pure type, an idealized family face beyond individual peculiarities. The type face could be used as a norm for seeing deviations in any individual

---

[46] 30 of the 48 photographs were gleaned from the Hamburg Professor, Wilh. Weygandt, *Atlas und Grundriss der Psychiatrie*, München: Lehmann, 1902. Further examples of Weygandt's descriptive psychiatry (with extraordinary photographs) in: *Lehrbuch der Nerven-und Geisteskrankheiten*, Hall: Marhold, 1935 and *Idiotie und Imbezilität*, Leipzig/Wien: Deutike, 1915. The 48 photographs and the rationale of their selection is discussed in English in L. Szondi, U. Moser & M. W. Webb, *The Szondi Test*, Philadelphia: Lippincott, 1959, pp. 3–21. Parallel series of images have been devised in other cultures, e.g., Fikry Farah, *Etudes comparatives d'une série japonaise parallèle à la série originale du Szondi-test*, Berne/Francfort: Publ. Univ. Europ. VI/14, 1975.

[47] Fr. Galton, "Composite Portraiture", Appendix A in his *Inquiries into Human Faculty* (1883), 2nd. ed. London: Dent Everyman, n.d.

or, because of the intensification of dominant traits, it produced an image of the family's degeneracy, the "skeleton in the cupboard".

Szondi's test asks us to choose among eight syndromes as archetypal modes of suffering; for in our mode of pathologizing so our life is styled. As Jung said, types and temperaments determine how we live our complexes.[48] The notion of basic types of archetypal suffering appears in the elements of Empedocles and Plato (Timaeus) which were modes of *pathos*, ways of being buffeted by fate, being moved by necessity. The four temperaments of humoural medicine are terms — choleric, melancholic, etc. — also derived from pathology. There too temperament determined the style of one's fate and diseases.

More specifically, Szondi, and Galton too, touch our theme because they stress that type is seen in the phenomenal face. Genotype is present in phenotype. In the words of Jungian language, for instance, "animus" is not only an opinionated complex reaction, or a figure in a dream. "Animus" is visible as a tautness in the mouth and voice, a pallid skin, a graceless tension in arms, neck, and shoulders, a driven, haunted expression. Moreover, the face is place of revelation of the family ghost, the ethnic shadow, the hereditary taint, the deepest secret — recessive and pathological.

Szondi's theory is elaborated with genetics and statistics, but Szondi's faces on which the whole work rests can be taken as a modern variety of Theophrastean characters, or overlarge figures such as we experience when reading the great nineteenth-century works of fiction or of psychiatry. These figures have overpowering reality so that we identify with them, and are at once drawn in to envisioning our lives in their terms. (Psychiatry books still have this effect; hence we can see our selves and others so much more vividly and convincingly by means of their diagnostic configurations, those 'syndromes' which are vivified personified images. Szondi insists this identification through pathology is material and literal; I am suggesting it is the power of the patholo-

---

[48] Jung too saw the temperaments or types more fundamental in choice-of-neurosis than the complexes (*CW* 6, 970, 927–30, 960–61) and his specific theory of psychopathology relates syndromes to typology.

gized image itself which evokes what he calls "psychoshock". Here we go back to the Art of Memory[49] and its idea that pathologized images are the most effective movers of the soul. But now we see that what moves the soul most is the "intolerable image" — the face of soft homosexuality, the face of brutal paroxysmal rage — which, because it is so deeply shocking, precisely constellates my repressions, and thus the turns of my fate, even to death.

Gestalt: Gestalt psychology has made us remember again that the whole world, and not only the human face, presents itself physiognomically. We perceive not just discrete particular sensations — green blotches, bird notes. We perceive significant whole patterns — the palm frond together with a bird's melody in which total physiognomy there are emotional qualities. And, it is not our subjective ability to empathize (Lipps) or our intentional set of mind (Brentano) that occasions these qualities; nor do we project them into the face of the world. They are there, given in the image. "Ein Ding", said Wertheimer, "ist so gut unheimlich, wie es schwarz ist, ja es ist in erster Linie unheimlich". Katz says: "Die physiognomischen Eigenschaften der Umgebung sind die primären, nicht die kognitiven. Und das gilt in gleicher Weise für leblose wie lebende Dinge."[50] A paper by Wertheimer in 1912 is said to be the official beginning of Gestalt psychology. So it begins during that period of fragmentation of forms that characterizes the consciousmess of many fields at the outbreak of the First World War.[51] (We shall come back to this period from quite a different angle later.) Gestalt attempted to deal with the dissociation by denying that consciousness was composed of associated particulars, the fragmen-

---

[49] F. A. Yates, *The Art of Memory*, London: Routledge, 1966, pp. 10, 109f, and as I discussed, *Eranos 37–1968*, pp. 333ff. The notion of the "intolerable image" comes from Rafael Lopez-Pedraza as developed in his *Hermes and His Children*, Zürich: Spring Publ., 1977.

[50] Both quotations from D. Katz, *Gestaltpsychologie* 4th ed., Basel/Stuttgart: Schwabe, 1969, p. 95.

[51] For a list of these many breakdown and breakthrough events in art, music, letters, science and especially psychology which occurred between 1911 and '14, see my *The Myth of Analysis*, pp. 164–65.

tation by insistence on wholes, the surrealist by promulgating laws, the schizophrenic by a religious isomorphism[52] which united mind, body, and world by means of forms. Its psychology of wholes bloomed at a time when things had fallen apart. So we can understand its having been acclaimed as a revolution of vision, even though Ernst Mach as far back as the 1860's had begun to show that a tree and a melody are perceived as wholes and not as composites of discrete pieces, and that we perceive two blotches of color differently according to their forms, i. e., we have sensations of a formal, spatial kind.[53]

Gestalt psychology contributes to an archetypal psychology of the image as significant form that precedes and is perhaps different from its cognitive meaning. A Gestalt view of the human image, or of any image, gets us beyond interpretations and out of the hermeneutic cages that have trapped our immediate perceptions.

Gestalt has observed that an image is *sinnträchtig*. We could reconsider this "physiognomic character" of an image to be what we call its "archetypal" quality. Then, the archetype would not be *behind* the image as a hypothetical noumenon in a Kantian sense, not a form to be inferred from or pieced together by amplification and resemblances, or to be experienced as an imperative through powerful affects.

---

[52] Isomorphism (Köhler, Koffka, Metzger) claims an inherent similarity between the *psychological* patterns in perception, physical patterns in the structures of things, and *physiological* patterns in the central nervous system. The great realms of being — anorganic nature, organic life, and conscious mind — meet in the C.N.S. There is one world united by forms: morphic monism. Isomorphism offers the religious doctrine of correspondences (Böhme, Ekkehart, Goethe) in scientific dress. Because of the new dress, the multiplicities in the old correspondence idea are forced into a unity (which then proliferate 114 laws of Gestalt). Instead of differentiating the faces of this unity, Gestalt abstracts forms and forces. Patterns lose their imagistic content becoming formal even mathematical structures. *Topos* becomes topology. Nonetheless the religious background remains in the Gestalt sense of mission. Karl Lashley called Köhler's work a "new religion", which Köhler willingly acknowledged in his *Die Aufgabe der Gestalt-Psychologie* (Germ. transl. of *The Task of Gestalt Psychology*), Berlin: de Gruyter, 1971, p. 37.

[53] Experiments with infants (between 4 days and six months) convincingly establish that form perception, especially the preference for representations of the human face over other patterns, is innate. R. L. Fantz, "The Origin of Form Perception", *Scientif. Amer.* (May), 1961.

Rather, the archetypal quality would be *in* the image as its significance, because, as the Gestaltists say, the image is itself "sinnträchtig"
(sense-carrying). Or, as Jung says:

> "Image and meaning are identical; and as the first takes shape, so the latter
> becomes clear. Actually, the pattern needs no interpretation: it portrays its
> own meaning" (*8*, §402).

We are now distinguishing between the *meaning* of an image and
its *significance*: the first is what we give to it; the second what it gives
to us. It bears the gift of significance; it is fecund with implications;
or, in Gestalt language, an image has pregnancy.[54] It carries within
its own body the potential of archetypal resonance. The archetype's
inherence in the image gives body to the image, the fecundity of carrying and giving birth to insights. The more we articulate its shape,
the less we need interpret.

To see the archetypal in an image is thus not a hermeneutic move.
It is an imagistic move. We amplify an image by means of myth in
order not to find its archetypal meaning but in order to feed it with
further images that increase its volume and depth and release its
fecundity. Hermeneutic amplifications in search of meaning take us
elsewhere, across cultures, looking for resemblances which neglect the
specifics of the actual image. Our move, which keeps archetypal significance limited within the actually presented image, also keeps meanings always precisely embodied. No longer would there be images
without meaning and meaning without images. The neurotic condition
that Jung so often referred to as "loss of meaning" would now be
understood as "loss of image", and the condition would be met therapeutically less by recourse to philosophy, religion, and wisdom, and
more by turning directly to one's actual images in which archetypal
significance resides.

Unless we maintain this distinction between inherent significance
and interpretative meaning, between insighting an image and herme-

---

[54] Susanne Langer, *Feeling and Form*, N. Y.: Scribner's, 1953, p. 8f, for a discussion of her "principle of fecundity".

neutics, we shall not be able to stay with the image and let it give us what it bears. We shall have the meaning and miss the experience, miss the uniqueness of what is there by our use of methods for uncovering what is not there. We shall forget that wholeness is not only a construction to be built or a goal to achieve, but, as Gestalt says, a whole is presented in the very physiognomy of each event.

But Gestalt psychology did not harvest what it had sown. Its work on the image became optics, and it never had much to say about individuality. It soon fell into the usual division of modern psychological thinking: on the one hand, seeking ever more general formulations, as if caught by its own doctrine of wholes, it became scientistically experimental developing 114 "laws" of Gestalten, with an algebra of forces, field theory, vectors, brain physiology, visual perception; on the other hand, it became Gestalt therapy — Fritz Perls, and groups. The "Good" Gestalt (Kurt Koffka), where good "means regular, symmetric, simple, uniform, closed, showing uniform direction — in short exhibiting the minimum possible amount of stress",[55] became both a law to be established experimentally and a psychological aim to be achieved therapeutically.

Nonetheless, Gestalt restores a Greek and religious way of viewing the world. The Greeks placed their sanctuaries according to the physiognomic character of the landscape: particular spots spoke to and of particular Gods.[56] The face of every event bears significance. To read the world, we must read its face, the presenting surface of its landscape and our inscape in response to it. We must stick to the image. That is where each particular wholeness lies. Unity is a quality given with the face of each event.

Lavater: Our next avenue again goes through Zürich, one of its most odd and most beloved natives: Johann Kaspar Lavater (1741—1801).

---

[55] Leonard Zusne, *Visual Perception of Form*, N. Y./London: Academic Press, p. 126.

[56] Cf. Paula Philippson, *Griechische Gottheiten in Ihren Landschaften*, Oslo: Brogger, 1939 and Vincent Scully, *The Earth, the Temple, and the Gods*, N. Y.: Praeger, 1969.

Although he was a friend or correspondent of the major figures of his age — Goethe, Moses Mendelssohn, Herder, Hamann, Fuseli, nobility and royalty — and though he preached and published a good deal of personal Protestant theology, he is known mainly for his *Essays on Physiognomy*, or as they were called in German, *Physiognomische Fragmente zur Beförderung der Menschenkenntnis und Menschenliebe*, published in four parts between 1775 and 1778.[57]

The first main thesis which Lavater's work tries to establish is much the same as that of Darwin and Gestalt psychology: the universality of physiognomics. His approach, however, is from the beginning *subjective*. Particular faces produce particular sensations in the onlooker, and "exactly similar sensations cannot be generated by faces that are in themselves different" (p. 31). Lavater extended his notion of 'face' also in the manner of the Gestaltists. All things have their physiognomic character:

> "Do we not daily judge of the sky by its physiognomy? No food, not a glass of wine, or beer, not a cup of coffee, or tea, comes to table, which is not judged by its physiognomy, its exterior; and of which we do not thence deduce some conclusion respecting its interior..." (p. 16).

Regional character also shows in the face. For example, of an engraving of a citizen of Zürich, he writes: "No Englishman looks thus, no Frenchman, no Italian, and, certainly, no citizen of Basel, or Bern."

Lavater also recapitulates the long tradition of comparison between animal and human faces and skulls, the major basis of Darwin's theory and also an idea that some have suggested goes back before Aristotle, before Babylonia, to animal totemism. Each kind of animal life bears its distinct nature in its form.

---

[57] My quotations are from the 12th edition of the English translation by Th. Holcroft, *Essays on Physiognomy designed to promote the knowledge and the love of mankind, to which are added One Hundred Physiognomical Rules (a posthumous work) and Memoirs of the Life of the Author, with 400 profiles and engravings* (London: Wm. Tegg, 1862).

"Were the lion and the lamb, for the first time, placed before us, had we never known such animals, never heard their names, still we could not resist the impression of the courage and strength of the one, or of the weakness and sufferance of the other." "As the make of each animal is distinct from all others, so, likewise is the character." "...the peculiar qualities of a species are expressed in the general form of that species" (p. 212).

Internal significance is revealed in self-portrayal; archetypal nature appears in the image itself. And so, it is the task of physiognomy to read the image, precisely, just as it appears.

It is the *structure* of the image that draws Lavater's eye. Unlike Darwin, Charles Bell, Duchenne,[58] and Piderit — all in the 19th century who interpreted the face's expression through movement of muscles, a functional, dynamic view — Lavater's eighteenth-century physiognomy searches out character at rest (p. 12); its concern is with essence not behavior; it is an examination of form, not expressive emotion, (*Wesenschau* not *Dynamik*).

Lavater too had his "good" Gestalten. His ideal form is a line that is neither too cramped and rigid, nor too soft and flexible, that line, *frei* and *richtig*, which drops like a string with a lead weight attached. This anchored lead-weighted image of the right line pendant with gravity, Lavater had engraved as an allegorical motto on a title page of his work.

The emphasis upon line shows that Lavater thought more as a calligrapher than did the Gestaltists. His was the eye that perceived more the handwriting of the creator — His signature in all things, rather than His geometry. God is more the artist who works in images, than he is the scientist who works through numbers and laws. The distinction between artist and scientist was applied to Lavater himself by his

---

[58] G. B. Duchenne, *Méchanisme de la physionomie humaine, ou Analyse électro-physiologique de l'expression des passions* (Paris, 1862). Before Darwin's major work, Duchenne had painstakingly elaborated a theory which correlated each muscle of the face with a specific passion; these muscles, being the same for all mankind, cause the universally instinctual facial language of emotion.

contemporaries.[59] And this Creator makes each individual different: "it is the first, the most profound, most secure, and unshaken foundation-stone of physiognomy that, however intimate the analogy and similarity of the innumerable forms of men, no two men can be found who, brought together, and accurately compared, will not appear to be very remarkably different" (p. 16). God as image-maker and man perceiving imaginatively contrast with God as law-maker and man perceived typologically. To the artist's idiographic eye, differences stand out; while to the rationalist's nomothetic eye it is similarities, classes, types. Neither Gall and his measurements of skulls, nor Carus and his idealized types or models were able to equal Lavater's imagistic eye for individual differences.[60]

In order to describe these individual differences Lavater insists that one be "inexhaustibly copious in language". He is forced by the immense subtlety of physiognomic expression to "be the creator of a new language" (p. 65). We are reminded of the 17,953 trait names mentioned earlier. Lavater says that poverty of language makes us unable to grasp what we see, perhaps even to see at all. We see what our language allows us to see, a statement drawing support from experimental studies which show a link between having the ability to be an accurate judge of personality and having artistic and literary interests.[61] I am suggesting that the substitution of clinical language for literary, of mathematical exactness for imaginative precision, the learning of observation through microscopic medicine rather than through bedside portraits and biography, and the reliance upon sociopsychological testing instead of moral-characterological scrutiny, has all contributed to our decline in psychological perception of the individual person, and thus to our age of psychopathy.

---

[59] Reinhard Kunz, *Johann Caspar Lavaters Physiognomielehre im Urteil von Haller, Zimmermann, und anderen zeitgenössichen Aerzten* (Diss. Univ. Zürich; Zürich-Juris, 1970).

[60] Cf. Ruth Züst, *Die Grundzüge der Physiognomik Johann Kaspar Lavaters* (Diss. Univ. Zürich; Bülach: Steinmann-Scheuchzer, 1948). pp. 98–100, for a comparison of Lavater's with other physiognomonics.

[61] P. E. Vernon, *Personality Assessment* (London: Methuen, 1964), pp. 68–69.

Lavater was well aware that nowhere perhaps are we more apt to project than when looking into the face of another person.[62] The problem of projection when trying to read another human being characterizes all modern psychology, which has devised its methods of distancing, objectivizing, and measuring to be sure that we do not form our judgments by subjective feelings. Yet these 'objective' measures to counteract projection seem to make psychologists such poor perceivers. A study by Estes in 1938, borne out by Luft in 1950 and by Taft after that, affirms that psychiatrists and clinical psychologists are inferior to artists, to laymen, and even to physicists as judges of personality![63]

Lavater's method for correcting projection was not by recourse to the scientistic distancing of objective techniques. His discipline was psychological:

---

[62] The "argument from projection" against physiognomics actually serves it: when we assume receding-chinned, sallow-complexioned, watery-eyed, thin-haired faces to be lacking in aggressive determination, and we find men, such as General James Wolfe the British hero of Quebec, to put the lie to this assumption ("projection"), whence does the stereotypic "projection" arise if not from the archetypal significance of these physiognomic traits by which we have read "weakness" in Wolfe's face? Cf. J. Brophy, *The Human Face Reconsidered* (London: Harrap, 1962), p. 164–86.

[63] Vernon, *loc. cit. sup.* with full references. The study by J. Luft, "Implicit Hypotheses and Clinical Predictions", *J. Abn. Soc. Psychol.* 45:1, 1950, pp. 756–59, attempted to measure how well clinicians understood a patient as compared with non-clinicians after listening to a case conference summary. "An analysis of variance failed to bring out significant differences between the clinical and non-clinical groups... the psychodiagnostician who had administered the Wechsler-Bellevue scale, the Rorschach, the TAT and one or two other tests, and, who was also present at the case conference, obtained a prediction score equivalent to chance". R. Taft, "The Ability to Judge People", *Psychol. Bull.* 52, 1955, pp. 12–13, writes: "...courses in psychology do not improve ability to judge others and there is considerable doubt whether professional psychologists show better ability to judge than do graduate students in psychology" ...however there is "clear evidence that good ability... was related to painting and dramatic avocations but not musical" ... "the ability to rate traits accurately and to predict... responses correlates positively with simple, traditional, artistic sensitivity." Moreover, both Luft and Taft report findings that show physical scientists to be significantly superior, as judges of others, to social scientists. R. Taft, "Some Characteristics of Good Judges of Others", *Brit. J. Psychol.* 47, 1956, p. 24.

"In proportion only as he knows himself will he be able to know others" (p. 66). "For this reason, the physiognomist must, if he knows himself, which he in justice ought to do before he attempts to know others, once more compare his remarks with his own peculiar mode of thinking, and separate those which are general from those which are individual, and appertain to himself" (p. 67). [Without this discipline of knowing his own heart,] "thou wilt read vices on that forehead whereon virtue is written and wilt accuse others of those failings and errors which thy own heart accuses thee. Whoever bears any resemblance to thine enemy will be accused of all those failings and vices with which thy enemy is loaded by thy own partiality and self-love" (p. 68).

Here is a Zürich precursor of the C. G. Jung who laid it strongly on Freud that the analyst be analyzed himself before attempting to work with others; the C. G. Jung who stressed that the projection of shadow is problematic in all human relationships.

We can learn from Lavater something about this shadow projection. He said: "Whoever does not, at the first aspect of any man, feel a certain emotion of affection or dislike, attraction or repulsion, never can become a physiognomist" (p. 63). Sympathy and antipathy are psychological tools; evidently, these gut reactions of the shadow help us perceive. To hold them off in the name of objectivity does not improve perception but falsifies it. So, too, we injure our perceptual ability by supposedly integrating the shadow. By this I mean that my intense feelings of repulsion and dislike about someone — Mr. Nixon say — are not only part of me to integrate. They are part of the percept of Mr. Nixon, part of his physiognomy and given with his Gestalt. The more I take the world in as my shadow to integrate, the less I can differentiatedly perceive the world's actual physiognomic character. To call a perception "shadow" generalizes the perception; we are no longer seeing but conceiving. If we do not trust our own eyes to see, and ears to hear, and to stand for what we feel when we see and hear, we then increase paranoid suspicions about what we are sensing. As our observational precision decreases, vague paranoid impressions veil us in. The task is age-old: to discern the Devil in his actual manifestations, rather than to theologize about sin. This does not mean that shadow emotions must be taken literally as truths about the object but neither are they to be taken as projections, pure subjectivities that belong only to me. Gut reactions are not general, but specific to speci-

fic 'faces'. They call for *precision*, which is neither integration nor
projection.

If in Darwin and Szondi genetic inheritance determines physiognomy, and in Gestalt psychology, topological laws, in Lavater it is
imagination that determines the visible form. Imagination in the
mother forms her child in the womb. Hyperactive imagination pro-
duces the giant and imagination in its passivity, the dwarf. "Imagination
acts upon our own countenance, rendering it in some measure resem-
bling the beloved or hated image, which is living, present, and fleeting
before us..." (p. 374). "The image of imagination often acts more
effectually than the real presence..." (p. 374). How did Jung put it?
"The psyche creates reality every day. The only expression I can use
for this activity is *fantasy*" (6, §78).

Man is created as an image, in an image, and by means of his images.
Therefore he appears first of all to the imagination so that the perception of personality is first of all an imaginative act (to which sensation, emotion, and ideation contribute but do not determine). Modern psychological methods of examining images and imagination in
terms of sensations or feelings start the wrong way around.[64] Since
imagination forms us into our images, to perceive a person's essence
we must look into his imagination and see what fantasy is creating his
reality. But to look into imagination we need to look with imagination,
imaginatively, searching for images with images. You are given to my
imagination by your image, the image of you in your heart as Michelangelo, as Neoplatonism, as Henry Corbin would say, and this image
is composed not only of wrinkles, muscles, and colours accreted
through your life, though they make their contribution to its complexity. To see you as you are is an imagination, as Lavater says, of structure, the divine image in which your essence is shaped.

We have now moved from persons as *faces* to persons as *images*.

The imaginative act of seeing requires, Lavater says, a variegated
language, self-discipline about projection (knowledge of my own heart

---

[64] This kind of approach is critically reviewed by Mary Watkins, *Waking
Dreams* (New York: Gordon & Breach, 1976), pp. 77–90.

and its images), experience of the world — and an eye that sees *instantaneity*. Here words reach their limit, for language must be strung into sentences. They proceed in time, forming narratives, stories. But the image is perceived all at once, as a Gestalt, all parts simultaneously.[65] In a letter — and now I am relying on a splendid early work of Ernst Benz[66] on Lavater and Swedenborg — Lavater says:

> "Every language of this world, even the most perfect, has an essential imperfection — that it is only successive: whereas the speech to the eye of images and signs is instantaneous. The language of Heaven in order to be perfect must be both successive and instantaneous. It must present a whole heap of images, thoughts, sensations, all at once like a painting, and yet also present their succession with the greatest speed and truthfulness. It must be painting and speech together" (from Benz, p. 199).

Lavater here is echoing a classical (Horace), and eighteenth-century, idea, "Ut pictura poesis": the formal and contentual unity of painting and poetry.[67] His vision is thoroughly spatial, and language cannot adequately speak of spatial relations because it talks in time. But Lavater is going beyond aesthetics; he is speaking of the language of Heaven, of angels to whom all is revealed in a flash, and who read the character of man, and judge him thereby, through his image. Here Lavater deepens Darwin. If the expression of man is transcultural and universal, then so must be the eye that reads the expression. As Gestalt psychology said physiognomics is primary and universal, and Darwin

---

[65] The contrast between image simultaneity and narrative succession, and the different psychological effects of the two modes, is developed by Patricia Berry, "An Approach to the Dream", *Spring 1974* (N. Y./Zürich: Spring Publ.), pp. 63, 68–71.

[66] Ernst Benz, *"Swedenborg und Lavater. Ueber die religiösen Grundlagen der Physiognomik"*, *Zeitschrift f. Kirchengeschichte* 57, 1938, pp. 153–216. Also, more penetratingly, E. Benz, "Die Signatur der Dinge: Aussen und Innen in der mystischen Kosmologie, in Schriftauslegung und Physiognomik" *Eranos 42-1973*, esp. pp. 553—79.

[67] Cf. R. G. Saisselin, "Ut Pictura Poesis" in his *The Rule of Reason and the Ruses of the Heart* (Cleveland: Case Western Reserve, 1970), pp. 216-24; Mario Praz, "Ut Pictura Poesis" in his *Mnemosyne* (Princeton: Princeton Univ., 1970), Chap. 1.

traced it to the universals of the animal primitivity of mankind, Lavater transforms primitive and primary to mean *a priori*, the "Ursprache of humanity", as Benz says. The image of man precedes the interpretation of man.

Moreover, Lavater continues, in the same passage (Brief 16, Bd. III, pp. 104—15; Benz, p. 201), the resurrected body will be wholly revealed in its image in which every physiognomic item of the person will express superbly what goes on in us without having to speak a word. Lavater has here moved physiognomics into an angelic mode of perception of the unique subtle body. And he suggests a way of understanding psychosomatic symptoms as expressions of an imagining body, which — because it is also a moral body and not merely physiological — must bring with them, these symptoms, feelings of guilt or sin. The 'last judgment' as the ultimate revelation of the shape of personality, the image in the heart on the body drawn, is always going on because it is eternal. To the watching angel the presentation of a self is in everyday life where we are being visibly created by our imaginings, which means we are not a product of external forces, not what we do or choose, not what we have stocked in inventory, nor does it matter in that ultimate revelation whether our imaginings proceed via intuition or extraversion or feeling. We are being judged in our images, which gives to the image and all our imaginings an extraordinary moral importance.

III. *Persons as Images*

Imagism: Lavater's prescription: "It must be painting and speech at one and the same instant", brings us to our last approach, Imagism, the school of poetry in the English-speaking world that appeared during the same crucial years in London, just before and during the First World War, as did Gestalt psychology in Berlin and Jung's *Symbole der Wandlung* in Zürich. Although Imagism was hardly a movement and it lasted briefly, most major poets in the English language since then were in it or affected by it.

In the words of Pound (1908), an aim of Imagism is: "To paint the world as I see it".[68] To put the concrete event as subjective experience into precise images. Imagism recapitulated several traditions: French symbolism, Japanese Haiku, Classical lyrics.

Here are a few lines from H. D., Hilda Doolittle, the Grecian purist of Imagism. She was first the fiancée of Pound in Philadelphia, then the central woman of the tiny London coterie, then an analysand of Freud's (she wrote beautifully of her analysis with him), and finally a person some of you may have known, for she lived many years in Küsnacht where she died in 1961. "Evadne"[69] (singing of being loved by Apollo):

His hair was crisp to my mouth
as the flower of the crocus,
across my cheek,
cool as the silver cress
on Erotes bank;
between my chin and throat
his mouth slipped over and over.

One of Pound's, "The Encounter":[70]

All the while they were talking the new morality
Her eyes explored me.
And when I arose to go
Her fingers were like the tissue
Of a Japanese paper napkin.

And a passage from early Eliot, "La Figlia che Piange":

Stand on the highest pavement of the stair —
Lean on a garden urn —
Weave, weave the sunlight in your hair,
So I would have had him leave,
So I would have had her stand and grieve.

---

[68] In a letter to William Carlos Williams (21 Oct. 1908), in *Imagist Poetry* (Peter Jones, ed.) London: Penguin, 1972, p. 16.

[69] *Collected Poems of H. D.*, N.Y., 1925. Quoted here from Vincent Quinn, *Hilda Doolittle (H.D.)*, N.Y.: Twayne, 1967, p. 49.

[70] *Lustra*, N. Y.: Knopf, 1917, pp. 52-3.

In these lines the image tells a story, is the story, and each love story
collapses into the instantaneity of the image. *Ut pictura poesis*; event
as tableau to be seen.[71] The surface, concrete and visible, implicates
invisible volume and depth like sculpture. Pound (1914) called Imagism: "Poetry where painting or sculpture seems as it were 'just
coming over into speech'."[72] To bring this out, a poem called "Au-
tumn" from William Carlos Williams:[73]

> A stand of people
> by an open
>
> grave underneath
> the heavy leaves
>
> celebrates
> the cut and fill
>
> for the new road
> where
>
> an old man
> on his knees
>
> reaps a basket-
> ful of
>
> matted grasses for
> his goats.

Here, people, open grave, new road, old man on his knees, grasses
and goat form a whole wanting nothing, a Gestalt that is a unique
perception, or *a perception that creates uniqueness*. It comes into
being with the perception, in the uniqueness of the image. To be is to
be perceived: *esse is percipi*. And now we begin to understand that
the act of imagistic perception does not merely see or reproduce a

---

[71] Cf. Michel Benamou, *Wallace Stevens and the Symbolist Imagination*, Chap. 1
"Poetry and Painting", (Princeton: Univ. Press, 1972).

[72] *Fortnightly Review*, Sept. 1914, p. 461, (in Jones, p. 21); see further: T. E.
Hulme, "this new verse resembles sculpture rather than music", (Jones, p. 38);
and my mention above of Michelangelo (poet and sculptor). Emphasis on sculpture
is emphasis on image, structure and space, rather than on line, story and time.

[73] From *The Collected Earlier Poems* (London: MacGibbon & Kee).

uniqueness that is there. Rather this act creates uniqueness by its imagistic mode of perception. Uniqueness is created by *poesis*, shaping images in words. But first the imagistic eye that sees in shapes. For images are not simply what we see; they are the way we see. Thus the perception of uniqueness begins in the eye that sees imagistically,[74] whereas the eye that sees by means of scientifically constructed types will always conceive uniqueness as a problem.

Lavater, his friends said, was an artist despite his system. One had to have "his eye and his heart"[75] — and that was his true method. Scientific method depends on repeatability; if an opus in science, an experiment say, can*not* be duplicated it loses validity. A depth psychology concerned with soul in its individuality cannot proceed as a science. Hence Jung's remark that individuality means the end of technique, the end of prediction and interpretation which also means the end of 'scientism'. In place of the scientific fantasy of method for psychology, I am suggesting the imagistic. Instead of measurement, precision. I am suggesting that we see the complex in the patient's image and not only adduce the complex from his material. But psychologists do not have to become artists and poets, literally. We need but see as if we were. And speak so.

"Go in fear of abstractions..." says Ezra Pound. "Use no adjective which does not reveal something..."[76] F. S. Flint says: "...no word that does not contribute to presentation..."[77] To find the words for your image I need Lavater's rich, variegated language, the Allport-Odbert list of 17,923 trait names. Our usual psychological language fails the precision of the image. What is revealed with such terms as "introvert" or "mother-complex"? Morever, these terms of typicality — unless imaged — bring further perceptions to a halt. Our language also fails the emotion. Hulme points out that emotions come in "stock

---

[74] "...an artist makes you realise with intensity... something which you actually did not perceive before". Hulme, *Speculations*, p. 168.

[75] A remark of Zimmermann's, quoted by Kunz, p. 31.

[76] From Ezra Pound, "A Few Don'ts by an Imagiste" in *Poetry* 1913, in Jones, "Appendices", pp. 129ff.

[77] F. S. Flint, *ibid*.

types" — anger, sorrow, enthusiasm — words which convey only "that part of the emotion which is common to all of us". Measurements of these emotions do not make the concepts or experiences more particular. Whereas art in images, defined by Hulme as "a passionate desire for accuracy"[78] presents each emotion precisely. Here image-speech takes precedence over emotion-speech. When we react to a dream image in terms of its emotions, or describe ourselves as "suicidal", "depressed", or "excited", we are again typifying, and moving away from the etching acid of the image.

Let us remember here that a complex presents itself first of all as a cluster of precise images revealed in instants of time in the word association test. In one of Jung's early experimental works (1905), he demonstrates a pregnancy-complex. But this has been adduced from the words: stork, bone-bed, flower, red, blood, pierce, heart (5, § 605). These words phrased by an Imagist or a Haiku writer would restore to the complex its imagistic precision.

Jung's "complex" and Pound's definition of Image and Lavater's "whole heap of images, thoughts, sensations, all at once" are all remarkably similar. Pound calls an Image, "that which presents an intellectual and emotional complex in an instant of time" ... "the Image is more than an Idea. It is a vortex or cluster of fused ideas and is endowed with energy" ... "a Vortex, from which and through which, and into which, ideas are constantly rushing."[79] Thus the movement, the dynamics, are *within* the complex and not only *between* complexes, as tensions of opposites told about in narrational sequences, stories that require arbitrary syntactical connectives which are unnecessary for reading an image where all is given at once.

The preference for image, for structure, for sculpture, does not imply a static psychology. Rather I am in search of a ground for psychodynamics other than narrational sequences; the battle of opposites,

---

[78] Hulme, *Speculations*, pp. 159–66.

[79] These definitions of Image by Pound come from his various writings and can all be found in Jones, pp. 32–41. Further on complex and image, see J. B. Harmer, *Victory in Limbo*: Imagism 1908–17, London: Secker & Warburg, 1975, pp. 164–68.

Vortex – whirling, whirlwind

stages in a process, the pilgrim, the hero, or the developing child
— which all keep us confined to an ego psychology. Moreover, the
dynamics of story become types — the typical motifs of fairy-tales,
the typical stages of emotion in Freud and Erikson, the typicalities of
individuation in religious disciplines. Actually, it is narrational pro-
cesses that are static: their typicalities can be interpreted and predicted. We know where they are headed. To conceive images as static is
to forget that they are numens that move. Charles Olson, a later poet
in this tradition, said: "One perception must immediately and directly
lead to a further perception... always, always one perception must
must must move instanter, on another."[80] Remember Lavater and his
insistence on instantaneity for reading the facial image. This is a kind
of movement that is not narrational, and the Imagists had no place
for narrative. "Indeed the great poems to come after the Imagist
period — Eliot's *The Waste Land* and *Four Quartets*; Pound's *Cantos*;
William's *Paterson* — contain no defining narrative."[81] The kind of
movement Olson urges is an inward deepening of the image, an insighting of the superimposed levels of significance within it.[82]

This is the very mode that Jung suggested for grasping dreams — not
as a sequence in time, but as revolving around a nodal complex.
If dreams, then why not the dreamers. We too are not only a sequence
in time, a process of individuation. We are also each an image of
individuality. We each turn in a vortex, and each movement in that
vortex, that complex, opens another perceptive insight, reveals another
face of our image.

---

[80] *The New American Poetry* (D. M. Allen, ed.) N.Y.: Evergreen, Grove, 1960,
pp. 387–88, from Jones, p. 42.

[81] Jones, p. 40.

[82] H. D. later turned narration itself into image by writing a novel in which the
stories were "compounded like faces seen one on top of another", or as she says
"superimposed on one another like a stack of photographic negatives" (Jones,
p. 42). Cf. Berry, p. 63: "An image is simultaneous. No part precedes or causes
another part, although all parts are involved with each other... We might imagine
the dream as a series of superimpositions, each event adding texture and thickening
to the rest".

Conclusions: Let us draw out several threads that have been running through our work this morning. First, we may reflect that typologies, for all their service in organizing a variegated world of multiple particulars, arise only in a mind that perceives the world in this way. "Chaos" and "order" lie in the eye that perceives as such. "Chaotic multiplicity", "bare particulars", "10,000 things" are not givens. They are abstract generalized images hermeneutically applied to the images that are given. The given itself is shaped; everything comes with a face. It is neither a given of nature nor an axiom of logic that the world *is* a chaotic mass of bare particulars, which then require typing. The world does, however, become such when we remove its face, when we remove its significant subjectivity. So, too, is each of us, each animal and plant, a mass of bare particulars when each is denied its physiognomic character, when stripped of its self-presentation, de-animated, de-personalized. Then we must typify to order our atomistic data, put the world back together again, and breathe some life into it by means of a constructed set of personified images which, we have suggested, types cannot live without. Despite Jung's statement that his typology is not a physiognomy, it is; for even his types could not leave their ground in descriptive exemplary images.

To follow this further: if a de-animated world requires typing, then when we type each other in psychology, are we not de-animating, de-souling? Are we not at the moment we perceive in terms of feeling and thinking, Gemini or Virgo, mesomorph or ectomorph, extravert or introvert, turning the world into a mass of bare particulars, a distribution of traits, a "more-or-less" without precision. "To be is to be perceived". When to-be-perceived as a type is to-be-perceived not as a face, then we are collected into rough-edged bins and roughly handled in terms of resemblance.

But notice here how resemblance is not conceived vertically, as an *epistrophé* in likeness to the image in which I am created and am continually being created. Instead resemblance — also in Wittgenstein's use of the idea — is conceived horizontally as a likeness to others across the sample. Conceptual types without images. Egalitarian. No longer am I the image I embody. I have become identified with what is not unique, my resemblance with others. My image has been fed to the type. My sense of image lost, my identity seeps out; and so I seem to have no specific shape that can be grasped individually.

Therefore, I become a problem. I must be interpreted and predicted about, requiring hermeneutic and scientific methods, and also psychological ego-strengthening to regain an identity that had been given with my image. Regardless of Christian faith in persons and philosophies of humanism and personalism, it is the loss of person *as image* which opens the door to collective techniques of handling persons. Persons in bins can resemble each other only in their commonality. So we would climb out into individualism by heroic acts of rugged will. Ego is the phantom risen, the idol erected, when the image cannot be seen.

Imagism has blessed the problem of this Tagung — Variety and Oneness — by cursing both its houses. We can see through both as fantasies of number. That polar construction between multiplicity *versus* the unit, unity, and oneness is again a typology which can seduce us from perceiving uniqueness. Both these fantasies of number, and the problem between them, arise when we do not stick to the immediately presented image whose anomaly is its integrity is its uniqueness. Uniqueness is anomalous; in our oddness is our integrity, our individuality.

Also the egalitarian-*versus*-elitism opposition arises from conceiving ourselves numerically, as units. Then to single out any one unit as unique creates an elite particular over and against the equality of the others. The mistake here lies in assuming that units, or bare particulars, are primary, whereas they are secondary numerical constructions. They result from a class concept — the unit — which has already egalitarianized uniqueness by reducing distinctions. Uniqueness is not a special kind of unit (CPID) that is different from all others, since each unit before it is classified as such is from the beginning different and unique.

Unity, too, need not be conceived numerically. Rather, we have been speaking of unity throughout as a quality of perception, the way in which each image is marked by the particular lines of its physiognomic character. Did not the Greek word *charassein* (from which "character" derives) originally describe the act of one who engraves or scratches marks or inflicts wounds. Where units may be added into larger unities, the specific markings that characterize each uniqueness have no common denominators. Oneness as a number dissolves into an image or into the quality of integrity given with each different image. With the dissolution of unity into a quality of the image, oneness can no longer be set up as a goal of integration. This goal is seductive only to its counterpart: ourselves conceived as uncharacterized, unimaged, unperceived units.

The character of uniqueness together with its painfully anomalous marks gives each person his or her integrity, his or her sense of being odd and unlike all others, and therefore irreplaceable. This further gives that dignity in the face of death which Unamuno calls the Tragic Sense of Life. The loss of any unit can be reproduced according to type or replaced by a spare part; the loss of uniqueness is irreversible.

Our second concluding thread draws out the animal analogy, opening the man-animal relation in a new way.

Modern psychology tries to reach the animal by getting inside its psyche. We try to imagine about animal perception, their images, language, and dreams. We have been anthropomorphic, attempting their consciousness in terms of ours.

Let us instead, by following physiognomics, attempt to perceive the animal in man — not merely in Darwin's and Lavater's sense of visible analogies. For what is being said in these theories is that there is an animal in man — an old religious idea (cf. *9, ii,* § 370); and we may look again at man theriomorphically, by which I do not mean merely genetically or in an evolutionary sense. I mean rather that the Gods themselves show their shapes the world over as animals, so that the animal is also an *imago dei*, a face of our eternal nature. By perceiving the animal in man we may perceive rudiments of divinity, essential archetypal modes of consciousness — leonine, hawklike, mousy, piggish — essential natures in the psyche that suppose paleolithic indelibility, and are our guardians.

The perspective I am suggesting here considers that the first psychological difference between humans and animals resides in how we regard each other. Humans regard animals differently than animals regard animals (and humans), so a first step in restoring Eden would be to regain the animal eye.

Here we are taking up Jung's idea — presented first at Eranos — that image and instinct are inseparable components of a single spectrum. As there are images in instincts, so we might say there are instincts in images. Images are bodies. Animal images in art, religion, and dreams are not merely depictions *of* animals. Animal images are also showing us images *as* animals, living beings that prowl and growl and must be nourished; the imagination, a great animal, a dragon under whose heaven we breathe its fire.

Darwin considered the animal *expression* in physiognomy to be primary. Gestalt responded by considering the animal *perception* of physiognomy to be primary.[83] If the world presents itself in expressive shapes like animals, then there must be an eye that can see shapes, as animals. To read lines on the face of the world we need an animal eye. This eye not only sees man as animal but by means of the animal, seeing each other with an animal eye. To this eye, image and type appear together. There is no abstraction of one from the other, no 'Ology'. As T. E. Hulme,[84] the Imagist, put it: "We must judge the world from the status of animals, leaving out 'Truth', etc." Wallace Stevens,[85] states in his poems that the animal is the first idea, the myth before the myth, whose perception is of physiognomic *Gestalt*, as a "lion roars at the enraging desert". This bird before the sun of our ordinary round and mind, this "dove in the belly" perceives, and

---

[83] Katz, p. 94, after reporting on experiments with animal patterns of recognition, then says: "Verständnis fremdseelischen Lebens muss etwas ganz Primitives sein... Ausdruck ist das allererste, was ein Wesen auf primitiver Erlebnisstufe von ausser ihm Seienden erfasst".

[84] Hulme, *Speculations*, p. 229.

[85] For some of these 'animals' in Stevens, see his "Notes toward a Supreme Fiction", "The Hermitage at the Centre", "Song of Fixed Accord", "The Dove in the Belly" in *The Collected Poems of Wallace Stevens*, N.Y.: Knopf, 1975.

creates with its response, the innate intelligibility of the world. This animal comes in our dreams, this animal — or is the dove an angel? — perceives *sub specie aeternitatis*, the brute eye that reads character in the flesh, and, like Lavater, instantly feels like and dislike. The animal eye perceives and reacts to the animal image in the other, the form which we display in our *Selbst-darstellung*.

Jung, by insisting on the archetypalness of images, Adolf Portmann by drawing us to the shape and self-display of life, and the Imagist poets have made it possible to perceive the brute world under our noses as distinct and unique images.[86] They show us the way of returning the natural world to its imaginal significance — the most difficult task for a mind that cuts itself off from the animal and thereafter divides the universe into mind (Hulme's "Truth, etc.") and nature, and then attempts to rejoin them by 'natural science'. Then the mind, pulling away from the divine sensate animal, our soul's protective angel, falls into the nature it would leave, but now mentally, putting the soul down into the scientistic, naturalistic fallacies.

Another thread is political. No governmental system depends more on the perception of the individual person by the individual person than does democracy. For what sense our vote if we cannot read the faces and voices and bodies of the candidates. Many millions cast their votes many times for Mr. Nixon despite the exposure for decades of his visual image. Does it help to analyze his personality, to find him an introverted thinking type, or anal, or paranoic-psychopathic, if we cannot see what is directly revealed? And evidently we cannot see, and so "people get", as Briand said, perhaps on this very lake,[86a] "the governments they deserve". We lose our ability to discriminate among qualities of men when we let slip the qualitative language for diffe-

---

[86] William Carlos Williams complains how difficult it is "lifting to the imagination those things which lie under the direct scrutiny of the senses, close to the nose... The senses [without imagination] witnessing what is immediately before them in detail see a quality which they cling to in despair, not knowing which way to turn. Thus the... natural or scientific array becomes fixed, the walking devil of modern life." ("Kora in Hell", *Imaginations*, p. 14).

[86a] i.e., the *Lago Maggiore* on the shores of which the *Eranos-Tagung* takes place.

rentiating personalities, for then how 'tell' one man from another, except grossly, roughly as demagogic pop-stars. Know your man by his decibel count. If even we psychologists trained to focus on individuality cannot, or dare not, discriminate, then how can we or dare we oppose the 'Ogical' views of man. If even psychology sees man as exemplifying typical functions, then there are no essential differences among human kind. We are functions, or functionaries, of groupings, an inventory of consumer tastes, actuarial probabilities, marketable skills, opinion.

Once a new Caesar had to exhibit himself, as Emperor Julian did to his troops, often and again, that he be seen, his person judged by his stance, his tone, his *Selbst-darstellung*. Once a candidate for admission to the Pythagorean academy was judged — not by a battery of psychological and intelligence tests — but Pythagoras, says Iamblichus,[87]

> "surveyed their unseasonable laughter, their silence, and their speaking... what their desires were, with whom they associated, how they conversed with them... He likewise surveyed their form, their mode of walking, and the whole motion of their body. Physiognomically also considering the natural indications of the frame, he made these out as manifest signs of the invisible manners of the soul."

The physiognomic eye could break the types into which we have been cast by concepts and statistics. Then I am no longer a typical intellectual, a typical Swiss, leptosome, Jungian, Jew, urbanite American, middle-class, or any of the other comforting places to shelter from the confrontation with me as a vivid calligraphic idiosyncrasy, an image close to your nose, with hands and handwriting, with gestures and intonations, eyes and mouth and creases, syntax and vocabulary, pelvis, gait, and skin-coloring, with a long ancestral history and biography of actions that present myself. Then the imagination

---

[87] Adapted from the Thomas Taylor translation of Iamblichus *Life of Pythagoras*, XVII, London: Watkins, 1965. Cf. R. A. Pack, "Physiognomonical Entrance Exams", *Classical J.* 31, 1935.

bewildered by this complexity searches for and seizes upon revelatory images to create a distinct individual.

However, by breaking the conceptual types, imagination re-uses them to feed the image. Typical perceptions of 'intellectual', 'Swiss', 'American', 'middle-class', 'Jungian', etc. — each a stereotype that sociologists abhor as prejudices, and psychologists condemn as shadow projections — return to narrow, limit, and add to the image the fixity of sculpture. Stereotypes solidify, as *stereos* means firm, solid. They fill in the type of a person with images of his ethnic, historical, psychiatric, and animal shadows. Stereotypes help us discriminate ancient depths of difference in visible surfaces, and Jung's old term 'racial unconscious' can be revived not in a literal genetic sense, but in this sense of shadow images that deepen our inner soil.

The seduction of typology goes further, you see, than the equalization of our external world. It is indeed no mere parlour game. It also flattens our inner perceptions of self — our dreams, complexes, behaviours. Our dreams become anxiety dreams or rebirth dreams, our complexes mother or father, our behaviours puer or animus. Types all. The archetypal persons become typological configurations, and the Gods dissolve again into the allegorical systems of the rationalizing mind, that iconoclast, that slayer of the dragon, that God-killer.

Not only is each person an image and this image is his invisible divinity presented, but each particular *aspect* of a person is a *face*, each face an *image*, this dream and this symptom, this behaviour and this desire, is also a distinct image, a tale condensed into a depiction, a visibility that needs no interpreted meaning, gives no certain feeling, a vortex that expands and solidifies a cluster of multiplicities rushing through it.

The image is itself — this room, you, others, me, the thigh on the hard chair, the attention fading in and out, appetite rising, the light through the leaves, palm rustlings and heat, stereotypically Eranos through forty years; yet, uninterpretable and unpredictable, a presentation, like an animal in its own display that is type and image at once and cannot go beyond itself, only deepen within itself; a presentation that sets limits to mind, keeps mind held within the image. As images are psychic reality and the source of every mental act, every meaning and feeling, so they are the dissolution of all mental acts, their end in image. Wallace Stevens said this in his late poem "Of Mere Being":[88]

> The palm at the end of the mind,
> Beyond the last thought, rises
> In the bronze distance,
>
> A gold-feathered bird
> Sings in the palm, without human meaning,
> Without human feeling, a foreign song.
>
> You know then that it is not reason
> That makes us happy or unhappy.
> The bird sings. Its feathers shine.
>
> The palm stands on the edge of space.
> The wind moves slowly in the branches.
> The bird's fire-fangled feathers dangle down.

---

[88] W. Stevens, *The Palm at the End of the Mind*, N.Y. Knopf, 1971, p. 398. The word "decor" appears in that version instead of "distance", see note, p. 404.